The Painted Ladies Revisited

Elizabeth Pomada
and
Michael Larsen

Photographs by
Douglas Keister

THE PAINTED LADIES REVISITED

San Francisco's Resplendent Victorians Inside and Out

E. P. Dutton

NEW YORK

(Left). 3755 20th Street. Portrait. Jim Lovegren found this unusual portrait of Queen Victoria and members of the royal family in an antiques shop in Dallas. The Queen is shown at her coronation, her Fiftieth Anniversary, and holding her great grandson, the Duke of York, along with her son, the Prince of Wales, and his son, Prince Edward. They are flanked by Alexandra, the Princess of Wales, and the young Duchess of York. We include this picture in homage to the remarkable monarch who gave birth to an era.

(Overleaf, page 2). 459 Ashbury. Doorway. This detail photograph shows the lavish use of gold leaf and the inspired use of color on the architectural details. The colors for the mosaic-tile paving leading to the front door were chosen to reflect the house's new colors. The entire house is illustrated on page 91.

(Opposite). 321 Castro between Market and State. Marbleized pastel columns in three colors give this delicious confection high eye-appeal. The entire house is illustrated on page 103.

(Overleaf, page 6). Western Addition #1. Front parlor. The owner of the house that contains this exemplary gilded overmantel of the 1880s collects a variety of things he enjoys: clocks, lamps, piano-roll music, and "a mishmash from the 1920s and 1930s." The overmantel was found at Butterfield's, and another rare find is the clock on the mantel: *Les Vendanges* by Rancoulet.

This book is dedicated to the artists, homeowners, painters, and color designers who are transforming San Francisco into the most colorful city in the world.

DUTTON STUDIO BOOKS/Published by the Penguin Group: Penguin Books USA Inc., 375 Hudson Street, New York, New York, 10014, U.S.A.; Penguin Books Ltd, 27 Wrights Lane, London W8 5TZ, England; Penguin Books Australia Ltd, Ringwood, Victoria, Australia; Penguin Books Canada Ltd, 2801 John Street, Markham, Ontario, Canada L3R 1B4; Penguin Books (N.Z.) Ltd, 182–190 Wairau Road, Auckland 10, New Zealand/ Penguin Books Ltd, Registered Offices: Harmondsworth, Middlesex, England./Published by Dutton Studio Books, an imprint of Penguin Books USA Inc./Copyright © Elizabeth Pomada and Michael Larsen, 1989./All rights reserved./Library of Congress Catalog Card Number: 89-50696./Printed and bound by Dai Nippon Printing Co., Ltd., Tokyo, Japan./Without limiting the rights under copyright reserved above, no part of this publication may be reproduced, stored in or introduced into a retrieval system, or transmitted, in any form, or by any means (electronic, mechanical, photocopying, recording, or otherwise), without the prior written permission of both the copyright owner and the publisher of the book./ISBN: 0-525-24812-9 (cloth); ISBN: 0-525-48508-2 (DP). 10 9 8 7 6 5

Contents

Acknowledgments

Helping to record the history of The Colorist Movement remains as much a labor of love and respect for us as it is for the homeowners and colorists who create the Painted Ladies. We feel very lucky to have the opportunity to recognize the artistry of these men and women.

This feeling is intensified when it's a homeowner. Recognizing the talent of homeowners—men and women who make their homes beautiful only for love, and who make us remember the meaning of the word amateur—is a special pleasure. Putting themselves on the line by putting their work on the street takes courage as well as art.

Working with the colorists and homeowners adds to the enjoyment of preparing these books. They are proud of their work and are eager to help. We would like to thank San Francisco's Victorian network for opening their hearts, homes, and address books in helping us to locate the town's most glorious Painted Ladies, inside and out.

Richard Zillman, friends in the Victorian Alliance, painters, and color designers offered suggestions.

Garden expert Roger Scharmer beat the bushes for us, as did Grace Hall of Thomas Church Landscaping, Theone Constantine, Annie Fine Chen, Tom Norwich, Katie Harmon, Alan Merbaum, Eunice Gomez, Andy and Karyn Sirkin and Laurie Paul, Anita Moran, Beau Gatewood, Jim Holland, Arch Wilson, Richard Reutlinger, and Bruce Bradbury. Antonia Anderson checked our prose and quotes.

For reviewing the manuscript and making helpful suggestions, our thanks to architectural historian Anne Bloomfield, editor Adele Horwitz, restoration architect Patrick McGrew, and historian and designer Paul Duchscherer.

Thanks also to John Mullane at the San Francisco Water Department, Ralph DuCasse and Tom Roberts, Gene McGraw, the Wilsons, Agnes Pritchard, Lesley Wilder, Toby Levine, Cynthia Baron, Frank Hernandez, Amelio Nurisso, Rose Huntington, Tom Molnero, Bill Grasse, Charles Edward Rappel, Joseph Biernacki, Emmett Walsh, Dale Seuss, Don and Wah Buckter, Pamela Smith, Tom Tate, Carol Malcolm, Bob Buckter, and Ron McCambridge.

824 Grove. Detail. This peacock, not an antique, usually perches at the far end of the dining room. We moved it so it could be better seen in all its multicolored glory. Peacocks and peacock feathers were popular in the Victorian era. The yellow silk chair is from a grouping that belonged to Sally Stanford, the legendary San Francisco madam who ultimately became the mayor of Sausalito.

Introduction-Hail the New Victorians

*"God took the beauty of the Bay of Naples, the Valley
of the Nile, the Swiss Alps, the Hudson River Valley,
rolled them into one and made San Francisco Bay."*
—Fiorello La Guardia
Mayor of New York City, 1934–1945

Welcome to the Golden Age of the Painted Ladies.
Lovers of gold leaf will pardon the pun, but this is the
most beautiful bevy of Painted Ladies yet. The
extraordinary beauty and variety of color, architecture,
and interior designs astonish us—and we live here.

When you see these houses, one at a time, spread out
across the city, they seem like gorgeous swatches in the
Victorian fabric of the city. Together, they form a
dazzling, irresistible tapestry.

When Paul Kensinger of Color Quest moved from
South Bend, Indiana, to San Francisco in 1975, he went
to the top of the hills overlooking Noe Valley, and he
saw a city that looked all white. Now, fourteen years
later, he says it looks like a Cézanne painting.

Painted Ladies, published in 1978, caught the city's
lovely ladies in the first blush of youth. They were
teenagers trying on their rouge and mascara for the first
time. It was the age of the "Hippie House" that was
painted in sixteen psychedelic colors.

The new generation of Painted Ladies that Doug
Keister has captured in his exquisite photographs were
shot a decade after *Painted Ladies* was published. Now
the Painted Ladies are ten years older and wiser. With
a couple of notable exceptions, such as Doug Butler's
purple passion at 1679 McAllister and Richard
Zillman's eye-popping circus wagon at 1189 Noe, wild
colors are now a part of San Francisco's ever-changing
aesthetic history.

But what has replaced them is a sophistication and
artistry that is breathtaking. The Colorist Movement
that started here in the sixties has emerged as a hopeful,
influential, socially valuable trend in American culture.
Why? Because these lovely Ladies give so much
pleasure that homeowners who see them want to create
one of their own.

The most enduring quality of the Painted Ladies is
their power of seduction. Seeing Painted Ladies stirs
the desire to create one. A continuing source of wonder
is that the desire to create Painted Ladies remains
contagious and that the movement continues to grow
spontaneously, not funded or directed by anyone but as
a labor of love, with respect for the architecture.

That the Colorist Movement spread from one city to
forty-six states and as far away as Australia in less than
a decade after *Painted Ladies* was published fills us
with anticipation for the future.

Cézanne City

Thousands of homeowners have transformed San
Francisco into the most colorful city in the world. If

there were a Nobel Prize for turning dead architecture
into works of art, it would go to the homeowners,
colorists, interior designers, and the craftspeople of San
Francisco.

The city's color starts with and is inspired by the
clarity of light created by the steady sea breeze and
brilliant sunshine. In Tennessee Williams's play
Camino Real, one of the characters says that blue is the
color of honor and of distance, an observation that
reminds us of San Francisco skies. You look up and you
see a brilliant blue backdrop, a flattering foil for the
Painted Ladies.

San Francisco is a unique and magnificent setting
that attracts creative people, people who take pleasure
in color and design, as well as artists of all kinds for
whom design and color are an essential part of their
personal and professional lives.

Bringing together a beautiful environment, creative
people, and people who thrive on color has produced
an explosion of color that is self-perpetuating.

The Grandmothers of the Movement

Color on the exterior of buildings is not new.

In the fifth century B.C. the Greeks built the
Parthenon on the Acropolis in glistening white Pentelic
marble. They decorated it with blue and red friezes, a
dusk-blue sky blazing with gold stars on the entrance
ceiling, and a pink roof. The huge marble statue of
Pallas Athena was painted in many colors and adorned
with gold.

The nineteenth-century American Victorian was a
pleasing, successful ensemble of warmth, color,
dignity, and good cheer. These homes are proof of the
pleasure their builders found in using new machine-
made building materials—from graceful cresting to an
orgy of jigsaw gingerbread.

The Age of Exploration

*"A true home should be called the noblest work of art
possible to human creatures…"*
—*House & Home Papers*, 1864, quoted in Allison Kyle
Leopold's splendid *Victorian Splendor*

Besides the inexorable momentum of America's
huge engine of commerce that has to keep producing
new products so that consumers will keep buying
them, part of the reason that color styles change is that
people like to experiment with color.

San Francisco shelters one of the world's greatest
collections of individualists. Homeowners are exploring the world of color, new subtlety in color schemes,
and greater attention to detail. They are experimenting
with gold leaf and silver and aluminum foil, new colors
of paint, and an exciting array of *faux* finishes that are
being used both inside and out.

In *Painted Ladies*, we called San Francisco an architectural museum, a statement for which this book once again provides abundant proof. What is new is that the fabulous color schemes on these buildings have turned the city into the world's biggest art museum.

Color designer Bob Buckter once said: "What I seek is rare beauty, and if I can't find it, I create it." When Bob got married early this year in the Green Room of the War Memorial Building, it was perfectly fitting that his wedding took place in the building that houses the Museum of Modern Art, for Bob and the other colorists whose work is represented in this book are artists.

They are artists whose work will be loved and respected a hundred years from now; in fact, as long as anyone else whose work is in the building. Their work started a trend that is preserving the landscape of Victorian America by transforming it with an inspired and inspiring marriage of art and architecture.

The big difference between the art in the museum and the art in the street may be that a hundred years from now, people will have a greater appreciation of the artistry of the colorists and the importance of their work in restoring the city's architectural heritage by reviving the century-old custom of celebrating with color what architects and carpenters created with wood.

Charles Dickens's novels were serialized in magazines, and millions of his devoted fans waited eagerly for the next weekly installment of *Oliver Twist*. Because his work was so easy to enjoy and so readily available, and because it's rarely possible to judge the enduring value of what is created before our eyes, few thought that readers would still be enjoying *Oliver Twist* 150 years later.

So it is with the art of the colorists. Their work is completely accessible, both in the sense of how visible it is and how easy it is to enjoy. How important can their art be if it's not in a museum, if it's springing up all around you in growing numbers, and if, in a nation where the chief cultural activity is shopping, it's free? All you have to do to experience the exhilaration of seeing three stories of colors that sing in harmony, are illuminated by a divine spotlight, and are framed by a glorious blue sky is go for a walk.

If you love color and Victorian architecture, roaming around San Francisco on a sunny day looking at Victorians is as close to heaven as you're going to get in this life. (Maybe someday Victorians won't die, they'll just be brought to San Francisco and turned into Painted Ladies!)

Granted that to see the Painted Ladies is to love them and to want to create one of your own, but could they really be *art*? Only time will tell. A show of forty images from our book *Daughters of Painted Ladies*, (1987), which opened at the Oakland (California) Museum, was presented by the U.S. Information Service in Brussels last spring and will be in Moscow next year. We hope that the show will continue to travel in America and abroad. Maybe like jazz, the Painted Ladies will have to travel abroad to gain artistic respectability.

A show of images from this book is also available. We are hoping to find a touring service to work with these and future shows.

We have been assured that the phrase *Painted Ladies* will appear in the next edition of the American Heritage Dictionary as the generic term for a polychrome Victorian. And a postal service that sees fit to commemorate the historical value of popcorn machines will sooner or later see the light and immortalize the Painted Ladies. Maybe your letter will help.

Mothers of the Movement

What was innovative in San Francisco two decades ago is now a tradition. At first, painting polychrome Victorians was a battle. Some people hated it; others loved it. But color caught everyone's attention.

White elephants were reborn with color and captured the whimsy and exuberance of Victorian architecture. As Ray Marchese said of his Honorable Mention home at 1056 Page: "The paint scheme resurrected the architecture."

San Francisco's Painted Ladies, the mothers of the Colorist Movement, are created by homeowners and colorists whose aesthetics—which historian Roger Moss calls the "boutique" approach—may be historically incorrect but do reflect the spirit of the times.

There has been much discussion about how to create a historically correct Painted Lady. There are two ways to do it. The most authentic is to use a scientific method to determine the original colors on the building and then re-create them as closely as possible using today's paint and materials. The other approach is simply to use colors and color placement that are historically correct for the building.

Some of the most beautiful Daughters of Painted Ladies, such as the domed octagon in Irvington-on-Hudson, New York, and the Morey Mansion in Redlands, California, are painted in their original colors.

The term *Painted Lady*—as it refers to polychrome Victorian houses—did not exist until the book was published in 1978. At that time, we said that the criteria for a Painted Lady were:

● That the Victorian building be a balanced, felicitous blend of color and architecture;

● That the house be painted in three or more contrasting colors;

● That color be used to bring out the decorative ruffles and flourishes.

We feel that, as in all things, people should trust their instincts about which approach is best for them and their houses. They can change their minds the next time they paint.

Keeping the Eleventh Commandment

Historian Kevin Starr describes early San Francisco as a camptown on a rocky promontory, cut off from land on three sides. The town sprang up overnight in 1849, and burned down six times before a fire department was formed. Pioneers who arrived with visions of gold dancing in their heads lived in hotels downtown near Portsmouth Square or around Telegraph Hill.

Gold brought riches and settlers with families who demanded houses at the same time that the Industrial Revolution was producing balloon-frame housing, machine-made nails, standardized paint colors, lithography for printing color charts, and catalogs of house plans and gingerbread. Northern California provided an abundant supply of redwood that was strong and long-lasting but soft enough to be spun into lacy ornamentation.

The city's population exploded from 57,000 to 233,000 between 1860 and 1880. In the 1870s, Italianate row houses blossomed with false fronts hiding gable roofs, with Corinthian columns flanking their entries.

The San Francisco Stick Style made its appearance in the 1880s. In this style, strips of wood outline the building, the bay windows, and the doorways. With enough gingerbread millwork, usually ordered from a catalog, the style was called "Stick/Eastlake."

(In his *Hints on Household Taste*, Charles Locke Eastlake prescribed simple lines in furniture, with form following function, but American builders did the opposite, layering more gingerbread on their Victorian homes. Then they added irony to insult by calling the new style "Eastlake"!)

The ultimate Victorians, the Queen Annes, with steep gabled roofs, shingled walls, arches, lacework, and sometimes turrets, marched up and down San Francisco hills in the 1890s. While façades varied, twenty-five-foot-wide lots were standard.

A local weekly emphasized the "striking variety" of the houses: "It would be difficult to classify these residences as belonging to any one style of architecture, for all the different orders have been reproduced with what might be termed a free treatment."

Of the almost 50,000 Victorians built up to 1906, only 13,437 survive: Half of them are victims of misguided modernization and the twin skin diseases, stucco and asbestos siding. The 1906 earthquake and fire, redevelopment in the Western Addition, and the lure of ambition and "progress" did in the rest.

By 1976, only 500 had been restored. In the last decade, that number has increased dramatically. Many of the 385 Queen Anne tower houses, 5,500 Queen Anne row houses, 3,600 San Francisco Stick style homes from the 1880s, and 3,100 Italianates and other buildings from the 1860s and 1870s are being given face-lifts, and springing phoenix-like back to life.

In 1884, *California Architect & Builders News* held a nationwide contest for designs for new residences. Although there were several hundred entries, the four winners all had towers and gabled roofs, frieze bands, and garlands of plaster, not wood. The Victorian house was whimsical with "inconsistencies, absurdities, oddities, and extreme fanatical tendencies." A critic attacked the gabled row house: "Man wishes an exceedingly active quality in his architecture. He wishes all parts of his building to be on the move—to be doing something—and he objects to the dignified surface and simple opening."

According to *Overland Monthly*, the misuse of ornament was especially conspicuous in San Francisco: with "a front loaded with endless repetitions of the same detail; the same scrawling scroll looking at us from a hundred window-heads; the same little panels stuck in every corner; strings of vegetables, all alike, hang from every column; and wreaths and cornucopias, badly carved, dangling between every projection, as if to leave a bit of plain surface anywhere were to break an eleventh commandment."

Others preened about "a showy house. This accomplished by a liberal plastering on of 'gingerbread' work and by engaging the services of painters who are expert in the mixing of fancy colors." These fancy colors were being bragged about in the *California Architects & Builders News* of April 1883.

After half a century of being smothered in Colonial Revival cheap white and surplus Navy gray paint, along with the dreaded stucco, asbestos siding, and other "remuddling" travesties, San Francisco awoke.

Some feel that The Colorist Movement began in 1963, when designer Butch Kardum dressed up his Italianate home in the Mission district. He quickly learned that a tasteful but colorful palette brought a heightened awareness and sense of pride to homeowners on the block.

Others feel that the "Hippie House" on Steiner, painted in psychedelic colors in 1967, sparked the revolution. At first, responses ranged from thankful to alarmed. Then the color generation married the preservation generation, those who wanted to live in town in a home of their own. When real estate moguls saw how valuable tattered Victorians could be, the wholesale bulldozing stopped. Neighborhoods came alive like turned-on Christmas trees.

The art of color consulting was born. After Butch Kardum came Bob Buckter & Friends, including Tony Canaletich, who later started San Francisco Renaissance; Tony's stepson, Ron McCambridge, who stepped out on his own to form Peacock Painting; and Bruce Nelson, who became Local Color.

They were joined by Joe Adamo, Robert Dufort of Magic Brush, Brian Moloney of Pago Painting, Jill Pilaroscia, and Paul Kensinger of Color Quest. Jill and Paul both started at Local Color.

The colorists didn't attempt to re-create history. They just wanted to design beautiful houses that pleased their clients. Around the country, dubious historians and preservationists quickly learned that color on Victorians could save them. Research has proved that San Francisco has always been unique, with a history of both fancy colors and exuberant trim.

West Meets East

"Let each dress worn by a lady be suitable to the occasion upon which she wears it...Never wear a dress

which is out of place or out of season...It is in as bad taste to receive your morning calls in an elaborate evening dress as it would be to attend a ball in your morning wrapper.

—*Ladies Book of Etiquette*, 1879

In 1989, the color tide is turning. "There's still less concern for historic accuracy in the West than there is in the East, but there is also less outrageous color. Designer Jill Pilaroscia, whose work appears on the cover of this book, says:

"People are looking for a more subtle, sophisticated, or unusual style. We take a contemporary approach, gleaning the best techniques from the past and combining them with imaginative solutions such as exterior stenciling, *trompe l'oeil*, and *faux* finishes.

"We seek a good look, rather than something simply bold or historic. The styles directly reflect what is seen in the best designer showrooms and architectural magazines. Homeowners are thirsting for contemporary looks. They are really thinking and examining new styles: Postmodern, Japanese, Pastels.

"There hasn't been a drop-off in desire, just a change in approach. It's a constant challenge for us to develop something that is unique and appropriate. Those really are the keys to designing color schemes in San Francisco today."

Ten years ago, some of the Painted Ladies in San Francisco were very loud. Now colorists and homeowners are more concerned that their color designs blend with their surroundings. Color schemes are subtler, but classier, more sophisticated, and more artistic.

Robert Dufort of Magic Brush believes colors change with time. "There's no question that we are seeing softer, more pastel colors being used in San Francisco. They used to be much bolder, but now they are becoming softer, more elegant. The same shift is happening on the interiors. Colors overall are becoming more feminine, less designed to reach out and grab your attention."

The new importance of color can be seen not just on Victorians. Skyscrapers are now designed in hues of rose, taupe, and turquoise. Office buildings are covered in *trompe l'oeil* "fool the eye" techniques. Older apartment buildings are being revivified with multihued color schemes. And the neo-Victorians popular with condominium builders across the country can be found on the streets of San Francisco. People feel comfortable with Victorian gingerbread even if it's new.

Tomorrow's Colors?

Yellows and browns, earth tones, were the colors of the seventies. People were earthy, folksy. Gray has been called the beige of the eighties. Grays and blues are cool; they go better with black and high-tech colors. Gray also changes with light to take on pink, mauve, beige, blue, or green tones.

Some color designers are trying dark, subtle schemes, with gold leaf for jewelry.

To understand the future, we have to look at the past. Roger W. Moss, co-author with his wife, Gail Caskey Winkler, of *Victorian Exterior Decoration* explains:

"The Color Movement is a reaction to the houses themselves; they just didn't look right painted white. As

Victoria Mews, at 20th Street and Wisconsin, is a two-block-square hamlet of offices and two-story condominiums that have borrowed the feeling, architectural detail, and color design of Victorian row houses.

The home at 717 Cole was once a proud Victorian like its neighbor at 721, which appears in the section on the Haight. The new owners chose not to strip the stucco off and go back to the beginning but to go forward. They simply painted on a whole new face by painting trim on the building.

The house at 2452 Washington is another "smothered" Victorian, on which the owners have lavished classical ornamentation, including Botticelli's Venus, that looks like it belongs on Italian ceramics. In our Mediterranean sunlight, this sunny house is like a little villa snuggled into a hillside on the Italian Riviera.

13

nineteenth-century architecture became more complex, colors began to darken and become more rich. They reached their richest darkest colors in the Stick Style and Queen Anne Style of the mid-1880s.

"After that, lighter colors came in with the Colonial Revivals: light blues, light gray, light yellow or white. When we got into the 1950s, when Colonial Revival became so popular as a suburban style, it was white, white, white. Now colors are getting darker and richer. It's the 1880s all over again, and we'll see colors continue to get richer for another five to ten years and then perhaps there will be another reaction. Design always runs in cycles like that."

The Old-House Journal editor Patricia Poore has observed: "Once upon a time, all old houses were painted white regardless of their vintage or size. That was a shame, not so much because it wasn't historically appropriate, but because a three-story Queen Anne tower house painted white looks hulking and pallid. Color it in and the same house arrests passersby with a display of texture, bold asymmetry and endless detail. The whole country is awakening to the creative possibilities of the Victorian palette…

"Yes, we should preserve good old work. And yes, we should respect the intention of the original builders. But the purists would have us freeze time, and turn our dwellings into museums. They forget that these houses were built by people who had everyday concerns with economy, comfort, and function, just as today. What makes preservationists think that history has ended? Why can't we make some history too? I say educate yourself, consider the long run, then give it your best shot."

A Thrill of Delight

Just as it is on exteriors, the Victorian spirit of play is also delightful in interiors. But homeowners have been using color to decorate the interior of their homes since prehistoric times. The caves of Lascaux, painted 15,000 years ago, still glow with twelve colors: yellow, two browns, two reds, two blacks, three shades of orange, ochre, and white.

These artists, who had the same qualities of perception, intellect, and feeling as we do, also had the good sense to live in one of the most beautiful places on the earth, the Valley of the Dordogne River in France.

They used coal, manganese-oxide, and iron oxide for blacks, and calcite and crushed shells for whites. Red was a mixture of iron salts, geothite, argite, and hematite. Today, we can go to a paint store and mix and match by computer. What's more important is the creativity we bring to making an art out of necessity.

In sharing the interiors of San Francisco's new Painted Ladies, we selected those created with taste, a strong sense of design, and attention to detail. In seeking the city's finest Victorian interiors, we found some houses that were stronger on the inside than the outside, so we have included them without their exteriors because we thought you would like to see them.

Some of the interiors shown are of the nineteenth century, some are of the twentieth century; and a couple—William Gatewood's and Richard Wagner's homes—transcend time with their owners' unique vision.

Many show the West Coast's Oriental influence. Curiously, the most authentic is not a museum but is a private home—Richard Reutlinger's home at 824 Grove. Most of them are Victorian in spirit. All of them are testaments to the love, pride, and dedication of their owners.

A hundred years ago, Victorians imitated everything, inside their homes and out. If they built a wooden Italianate, the exterior frequently looked like stone. Brass imitated gold. Machine-made imitated handmade. Plaster was given a ceramic, metallic, or wood finish. Pine was grained to look like mahogany or oak. You should decide how closely you want to imitate what was an imitation to begin with.

A century ago, Christopher Dresser told us in *The Art of Decorative Design*: "It invests a new charm, as colour bestows upon the flower a new loveliness. Beauty is that quality of an object which causes delight, gladsomeness, or satisfaction to spring up within the beholder or induces a thrill of delight in the soul."

At about the same time, a book called *American Victorian Interior Decoration* remarked on "a growing taste for color which is not satisfied with plain surfaces of one uniform tint, but demands from the decorator a well-arranged combination of many colors."

Designers were encouraged to use texture and something called "bloom"—a sheen made by metallic ink, pigments or pieces of stone, such as mica, which capture light and change the way patterns look at different times, such as by candlelight or daylight. Bronze powder and green arsenic had different qualities of brilliance. Flocking, embossing, mica, and powdered gold leaf were popular.

When More Was More

Author Allison Kyle Leopold feels that Victorian decoration and adornment were undertaken with a determination that bordered on evangelistic fervor. The time, energy, and money Victorians lavished on decoration was unprecedented. Artists and craftsmen in wood, metal, glass, upholstery, curtains, paint, and paper worked feverishly to fulfill the new desire for domestic comfort and romantic shadows.

The American Victorian home was a sanctuary, a nurturing oasis. Family photographs and memorabilia surrounded Victorians and gave them comfort. Rich color; flamboyant patterns and prints; jungles of plants; layers of curtains, shawls, and carpets; and travel souvenirs also helped homeowners show off their new wealth. As façades were embellished by gingerbread, interiors were also feasts for the senses.

The Victorian look is achieved by an accumulative process of adding more and more physical and psychological comfort to every room. "The Victorians liked an ostentatious show of possessions, and that is exactly the look I've created," explains Richard Reutlinger, who has spent more than a quarter century assembling the makings for the most remarkable Victorian interior in San Francisco in his home in the Western Addition.

By the middle of the 1800s, however, excess had become a hodgepodge, and leaders of the Aesthetic Movement, led by William Morris, John Ruskin, and James Abbott McNeill Whistler, sought to curb ugliness and inspire an appreciation of taste, beauty, refinement, and "art" in everyday living. New, acidic, "natural" colors were called for, but still few flat surfaces were left plain. Flowers and figures covered everything.

The Gilded Age

"Ornament is a thing to be desired, but to be desired it must be good, and it must be in its place."
—*House Beautiful*, 1877

Victorian homes have marked similarities: high ceilings, gleaming wood floors, vintage mantels decorated with tile work, pocket doors dividing front and back parlors, painted or stained woodwork, ornate furniture, and eclectic collections of art and figurines in all periods and styles, from ancient Egyptian to Federal to Art Nouveau.

Hallways give the visitor the first impression of the house, and decoration there was simple but significant.

The drawing room, or front parlor, had to be more beautiful and elegant than any other room in the house. The spirit of welcome and gaiety were the hallmarks of a proper parlor. Since the room was used only for important guests, the most cherished pieces of art and furniture were proudly displayed there.

Masculine in feeling, the library was a quiet retreat for study and contemplation amid rich, warm colors.

Meals brought the family together. Although the dining room, too, was thought to be masculine, it was also supposed to be substantial and elegant. Decorative paper lined the walls and ceiling. The focus of the room was a chandelier over an extendable table, centered on a colorful rug on patterned parquet floors. Candelabra of glass, brass, or silver graced the white lace or embroidered tablecloth. Sideboards were used for breakfast buffets, and to display prized china and silver. Mirrors brightened the room yet didn't distract from the food.

Lace curtains covered every window. Belgian nuns tatted lace curtains for mansions, but machines made them possible for everyone. Puddling the extra lengths of lace curtain on the floor was a typical flourish. The Victorian homemaker then added multiple layers of borders, heavy insulating drapes, a window shade, blinds or shutters, tassels, and fringes.

Continuing the layered look, carpets rested on wood floors, or fine rugs were laid on top of wall-to-wall carpet, which was usually patterned in vivid colors.

The Gilded Age glittered and glowed at night, with shimmering wallpapers and carved and painted moldings catching the soft yellow-red light from new gas and kerosene lamps. Chandeliers were used, with wall sconces and standing lamps providing additional light. Shades trimmed in silk, lace, beads, and ribbons were made of paper, brass, bronze, silver, crystal, tin, and Tiffany glass. But before the Victorian Age ended, homes went from romantic candlepower to the harsh white light of the new century: electricity.

Bedrooms were chaste and cheerful. Colors were lighter, airier, and woodwork was never white but painted to harmonize with the room's furnishings. The bedroom suite formed the focus of the room, surrounded by plants, pictures, a firescreen, and washstand with bowl and pitcher.

Ceilings were painted or papered in predominantly lighter tints and centered on the molded rosette "holding" the chandelier.

The Walls Around Us

Since earliest times, walls have been covered by everything from animal hides to tapestries for beauty as well as warmth. As wool was replaced by silk, so silk has been replaced by paper. It was the Chinese who first made wallpaper with carved woodblocks, which imitated Chinese painting and embroidery. By the late nineteenth century, paper was being designed by artists such as Louis Comfort Tiffany and Candace Wheeler in the East, and William Morris in England.

Many of today's papers are reproductions of Chinese art. Ornamental patterns, imitation textiles, and reproductions of trellises and gardens are available. Today you can cover your walls with commercial machine-printed paper that sells for $9 to $25 per roll, which will cover 36 square feet, or choose hand silk-screened, hand-blocked, or hand-painted papers with prices ranging up to $1,500 per running foot.

Bruce Bradbury, the high priest of fine High Victorian wallpapers, has been successful in erasing white from Victorian interiors. He has found that the same homeowners who tirelessly strip asbestos siding from their façades and painstakingly replace their lost ornamentation often treat the insides of their houses with a modernist vengeance, obliterating the harmonious proportions of their interiors in a white swath.

He points out that since nineteenth-century photographs are usually black and white or sepia, you cannot see the cornice that really has ten subtle variations in hue and value, or a door and its surrounding molding with up to thirteen closely balanced colors, threaded with pinstripes of vermilion or metallic gold. Ceilings were usually papered or painted cream, hazy blue, yellow, or salmon and centered by multicolor crown decorations. Multicolor, multipatterned papers usually covered the walls.

The red-flocked wallpaper seen in movies is a Hollywood invention, and until the 1890s, white, imitating plaster, was used only for the servants' rooms or perhaps a bathroom. Ceiling, moldings, picture and porch-railings, friezes, borders, dados, and polychromed cornices can blend harmoniously regardless of the multitude of colors or patterns. For example, Louis Sullivan's ceiling for the Chicago Stock Exchange incorporates a palette of up to fifty-two colors.

The mission of Bradbury & Bradbury Art Wallpapers is to revive the ideal of the nineteenth-century Aesthetic Movement. Bruce and his colleagues have taught the new Victorians across the country how to integrate a rich, sophisticated, highly personal form of interior ornamentation with the period and proportions of their homes.

"People are tired of unadorned space. It's a horror of the vacuum," Bradbury explains. "Today's Victorian walls are visual." Paint, plaster, woodwork, *trompe l'oeil, faux* finishes, abstract and figurative patterns, stencils, embossed Lincrusta, and decorative painting save us from the melancholy of white, blank walls. Like a beautiful exterior color scheme, vivid, elaborate interior wall decorations make you feel good.

Talking Flowers

Wallpaper patterns brought the outdoors inside. Living ivy was used inside the home, curling around columns and window frames in natural patterns. Outside, Victorian gardens were planted and pruned in bold color contrasts to resemble Oriental carpets.

Mixed borders combined shrubs, grasses, and flowering annuals and perennials. Urns and statuary added the proper busy touch. Dwarf edging, lavender, roses, alyssum, campanula, lilies, verbena, Sweet William, dahlias, geraniums, poppies, and spirea were popular. Strong contrasting colors were favored in porcelain and clear glass vases. The romantic, sentimental "language of flowers" influenced what Victorians grew and gave as presents.

A Search for Spirituality

In San Francisco today a lushness, a Victorian profusion of possessions and decoration, can be found inside many Painted Ladies. As it was a century ago, the eclectic, bizarre, or fanciful are "in." Paige Rense, editor of *Architectural Digest*, has written: "What we're looking for in interiors is a search for spirituality…people want interiors to nourish them, to give them something emotionally, intellectually, spiritually." We hope that like the exteriors, the interiors depicted here will nourish and inspire you.

Our Victorian buildings are a national treasure, a rich heritage of craftmanship we shall not see again. People seek out their past because it is through developing an understanding of the way things were that an individual can maintain a sense of self-worth today. San Francisco's Painted Ladies glorify our past and give us hope for our future.

A Note About the Captions

The captions include the address; the cross streets, to encourage you to explore; the year the house was built; and the architectural style of the house.

When we know who did the color design, the designer's name is given. To protect their privacy, the owners of some of the houses preferred to remain anonymous.

Most of the houses were built in one of the three basic San Francisco architectural styles: Italianate, Stick or Stick/Eastlake, and Queen Anne. But San Franciscans blended styles and added ornamentation if they felt like it. Some of the houses are transitional, incorporating features from a current style and a new style, such as Colonial Revival, that was just beginning to become popular.

The four sources we used for construction dates were homeowners; the two essential guides to the city's Victorians—*Here Today: San Francisco's Architectural Heritage* by The Junior League of San Francisco, Inc., and *Victoria's Legacy: Tours of San Francisco Bay Area Architecture* by Judith Lynch Waldhorn and Sally B. Woodbridge—and the Water Department.

The books didn't have every date and many of the houses have changed owners often enough so that the history of the houses has been lost in the shuffle. Many city records were destroyed in the 1906 earthquake, making it difficult to find dates. In these cases, we have added a (W) to the date to indicate the date when the Water Department turned on the water. However, some properties had their own well, spring, or cistern, which they used for years before the house was hooked up to city water. On other blocks, row-house contractors obtained water hookups before they built their houses.

Also, the numbers on some houses have been changed, and houses and blocks have been moved. And in a town where shacks were built on tent stands, cottages replaced shacks, and formal houses replaced cottages, the year a house was built may be open to question. In San Francisco, few street signs specify streets or avenues, with the exception of Chinatown's Grant Avenue and the numbered streets and avenues. Unless indicated, all the addresses named are streets.

Beyond these basics, we tried to include what we thought you would want to know about the history and the owners of these homes and what you would enjoy learning about them.

DOWNTOWN

After the Gold Rush in 1848, the most important event in the city's history took place shortly after 5:00 A.M. on the morning of April 18, 1906. It lasted forty-eight seconds and would have registered 8.25 on the Richter scale.

The worst damage that the earthquake itself caused was the destruction of the water mains and pipes and gas lines, because the broken conduits made it impossible to fight the fires caused by the earthquake. This resulted in a conflagration that destroyed downtown San Francisco.

The city was rebuilt after the shocker, but in later architectural styles. For example, the homes at 1029 Jones, 2228 Jones, and 547 Lombard are representative of the Edwardian style, which retained Victorian decorative elements but was more restrained in style. These Edwardians look lovely in their new finery. Edwardian is a term used only in San Francisco for Victorian-looking houses built during the reign of King Edward VII, 1901-1910. Some were built until 1915.

Downtown San Francisco is bounded by Market Street, Van Ness Avenue, and the Bay. Shaped like a slice of pie, this wedge of the city contains twelve distinct areas: Union Square, the Financial District, Chinatown, Jackson Square, North Beach, Telegraph Hill, Fisherman's Wharf and the Waterfront, Russian Hill, Nob Hill, Polk Gulch, the Tenderloin, and Civic Center.

While you are in North Beach, stop for a coffee at Caffe Roma at 414 Columbus, an odd-shaped work of art, and browse at the City Lights bookstore two blocks away at 261 Columbus, a literary landmark that was the unofficial headquarters of the Beat Generation.

Painted Ladies included only one house in the book that was downtown. We are pleased that there are now enough Painted Ladies downtown to warrant a separate section in this book. We hope that this will inspire enough homeowners so that next time this section will be larger.

547–49 Lombard between Powell and Stockton. 1908. Edwardian. A year after the 1906 earthquake, a reporter described the Latin Quarter or Italian section as "entirely rebuilt, with its gaily coated houses painting the landscape with crimson, ochre, emerald, cobalt, rose madder, and snow white, laid on in wide washes."

This extravagant paint job was the first home designed by Bill Weber and Tony Klaas of Mirage Painting. It's one of three artistic gems that Mirage has enlivened North Beach with. The other two are their spectacular murals at the corner of Columbus and Broadway (owned by the man who owns 547 Lombard) and on Green Street between Stockton and Grant. Visitors can see this home on the tour bus route to Coit Tower, which itself is worth visiting for one of the most beautiful views on the planet as well as for the WPA murals.

547–49 Lombard. Detail. Two patterns of marbleizing, one black with white veins and one white with gray and green veins, add visual interest to this entranceway. Mirage combined light, medium, and dark blue, brown, black, white, grape, and gold to make artistic magic.

1029–33 Jones between California and Pine. 1907. Edwardian. Nob Hill is where the Gold Rush millionaires built their mansions. The one remaining example is the Flood Mansion, a city landmark that is now a private club, a block and a half away from this house at the corner of California and Mason. Some say that the letter *s* was dropped from the word *snob* to create the name of the hill, but Nob is a contraction of *nabob*, meaning an Indian prince.

A former rooming house on one of the city's ten steepest streets, this set of three flats was built just after the earthquake. Bob Buckter created the quiet but contrasty design, following the owners' request for a formal, dignified look. Cal Crew applied the six colors.

Allyn and Mary Morris own the building next door, an identical but stripped-down version of 1029. Allyn's late mother, Pauline, owned both buildings, which had been rooming houses for half a century. One of California's finest architects, Allyn is based in Pasadena and has prepared a scheme of vivid primary colors for the house. Perhaps it will be on the house by the time you see it.

At the corner of California and Jones is one of the most beautiful churches in the hemisphere, Grace Cathedral.

769–71 Francisco between Jones and Leavenworth. 1899. Queen Anne row house. Colorists don't often go to the trouble to use six colors and hide three of them, but Clark Chelsey of Chelsey Painting did. From a distance, this house looks as if it has only three colors—light and dark gray and white, which has been cunningly used to pick out the scrumptious gingerbread. Closer inspection reveals navy, gold, and maroon accents, making for a classy, low-key, yet high-contrast scheme.

2228–36 Jones between Greenwich and Lombard. 1906. Edwardian. Bob Buckter worked with the owners on this stately symphony of gray-greens punctuated by burgundy. In their helpful guide, *Victoria's Legacy*, Judith Lynch Waldhorn and Sally Woodbridge describe this kind of house: "Some Edwardians have exterior stairs forming a series of balconies in the center of the front of the building; apartments in this type of Edwardian were called 'Romeo' or 'Romeo and Juliet' apartments because of the balconies, and because the small size of the units made them appropriate for newlyweds but too small once the first baby arrived."

In a neighborhood once populated by Italian fishermen, we're sure that these balconies, with their unique columns and balustrades, framed many a love scene.

PACIFIC HEIGHTS

With its luxurious homes designed in a range of architectural styles and its panoramic vistas of the Golden Gate and Marin headlands, Pacific Heights is one of the city's most prestigious and historic residential areas.

From the 1870s to early 1900s, this part of town was distinguished by large single-family dwellings on corner lots with relatively modest row houses in between. From the turn of the century through the 1930s, many of these residences were replaced by more luxurious houses in styles popular at that time. Another architectural wave in the same era brought apartment buildings, often with each unit occupying a whole story.

The queen of Pacific Heights is the Haas-Lilienthal house at 2007 Franklin, one of the finest Victorians in the city. The headquarters of the Foundation for San Francisco's Architectural Heritage, the house is furnished and a must-see attraction. The Victorian Guide in the back of the book has tour information.

For an enjoyable detour, take a walk on Fillmore from Sutter to Clay. Browser Books and Sweet Inspiration, at 2123 Fillmore, are our two favorite stops. On Union Street, try Solar Lights Books at 2068 and the Coffee Cantata at 2030.

Locals call the area from Sutter to California Baja Pacific Heights, but for the purposes of the book, Pacific Heights runs from Sutter Street to the Bay and from Van Ness Avenue to Presidio Avenue. This area encompasses the Marina and Cow Hollow, the area adjacent to Union Street that once boasted the city's dairy farms.

(Above left). 2919 Octavia between Filbert and Greenwich. 1895(W). Queen Anne cottage. Owners artist-sculptor James Lofrano and his wife, Sharon, restored, designed, and painted this charming cottage, which Jim's grandmother bought in 1924. Jim carefully picked out the dentils in two colors and is planning to replace the spindles, which his uncle took out before World War I because they were too much trouble to paint.

(Above right). 2965 Laguna at the corner of Filbert. 1890(W). Stick/Eastlake. Detail. An understated but effective Bob Buckter scheme illuminates the distinctive ornamentation on this bay window, which is a block away from trendy Union Street. In a fitting fate for a Painted Lady, the bottom floor of this chic Victorian has been reborn as Suit Yourself, a woman's clothing store.

(Left). 2806 Laguna between Green and Union. 1900. San Francisco Stick. The Victorian spirit of play is alive in San Francisco. The imaginative owner of this small home picked seven colors, then numbered the sections to be painted in a tongue-in-cheek paint-by-numbers color scheme. It's titled "Self-Portrait 1982." The paint was weathering when this photograph was taken, so perhaps by the time you arrive the numbers will be filled in.

2000 Pacific at the corner of Octavia. 1894. Colonial towered Queen Anne. This grande dame survived because its previous owners were grande dames: the Woods sisters, who lived here from 1919 to 1975. For its present owners, this stately home has been a labor of love, time, money, and effort. When they bought the house—the only old house left on their side of the street—in 1975, it needed to be completely restored. Using *The Old-House Journal* to guide them, and redoing a room a year, they finished a decade later and invited the workers and suppliers who helped them restore the house to help them celebrate its completion.

Like Linda Blacketer at 1556 Revere in the Bayview District, the owners donated a preservation easement to the Foundation for San Francisco's Architectural Heritage. This gave them a tax break, in exchange for which they and future owners are forbidden to change the façade of the house.

Since one of the highlights of the interior is its gorgeous golden-oak woodwork, the owners wanted earthy colors for the exterior. They wanted to strike a harmonious balance between a modern approach to painting the house and respect for the integrity of the architecture.

Because their home is large and on a highly visible street corner, they also felt the need for restraint. They chose green for the body color because scraping the back of the house revealed a similar gray-green as the original color. The Bob Buckter design complements the other homes in this quiet neighborhood.

Robert Dufort and Magic Brush received honorable mention in the "Picture-It-Painted-Professionally" contest sponsored annually by the National Paint & Coatings Association for the quality of their restoration.

(Above). Pacific Heights. Dining room. This gracious dining room overlooks San Francisco Bay. The elaborately carved built-in china closet, with thistley, Louis Sullivanesque carving, showcases the family dinnerware.

(Opposite). Pacific Heights. Fireplace. This glorious white–and–gold–leaf fireplace looks like it belongs in a Baroque church. Using dental tools on the fine details buried beneath eight coats of paint, the owners stripped the fireplace and in the process discovered traces of gold leaf.

The fireplace is made of a kind of forerunner of plastic made of plaster and sawdust poured into a mold. The grate, which the owners found at Butterfield & Butterfield, a popular auction house, is 200 years old and has been brass-plated. The dolphins on the tiles over the fireplace and the alabaster columns, topped by busts of mythical female figures, help make this fireplace a work of art.

(Below). Pacific Heights. Library. The owners adopted the Victorian tradition of creating a Turkish or Moorish hideaway. Picking a design from the book *Arabic Art in Color*, they used seven colors to bring the design to life.

For a year and a half, on weekends and vacations, they painted one color at a time. They couldn't tell how the room would look until they were finished. When they finished the room in 1981, well-known stencil artist Larry Boyce of Artistic License came in, lay down on the floor, looked up at their handiwork and said: "Eight thousand dollars." Diana the Huntress portrayed in the tiles over the fireplace adds to the room's Mediterranean flavor.

(*Opposite*). 2026 California between Octavia and Laguna. 1878. Italianate with curved glass bays. The family who moved into the house shortly after the 1906 earthquake added a fashionable bay, an Edwardian staircase in the hallway, and the stained glass in the stairwell.

Bert Franklin, an artist and interior designer who specializes in commercial spaces, took over in 1969, the third owner in almost a century, and gave the house a new look with a design of Thalo Blue, bronze, and white.

Next door, looking as wonderful as it did in 1977, is 2022 California, the house that is illustrated on the back cover of *Painted Ladies*.

(*Right*). 2026 California. Detail. The idealized Egyptian head that greets visitors and guards the portals to the house is the first of this house's three Egyptian treats.

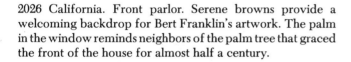

2026 California. Front parlor. Serene browns provide a welcoming backdrop for Bert Franklin's artwork. The palm in the window reminds neighbors of the palm tree that graced the front of the house for almost half a century.

2026 California. Back parlor dining room. The colors used in the front parlor, terra-cotta walls with a dark chocolate ceiling, are reversed in the back parlor. The gazebo in the rear, seen through the side door, is one of the few remaining 1890s gazebos.

Note the compact kitchen tucked under the staircase. The discovery of King Tutankhamen's tomb in 1922 unleashed a wave of Egyptiana, including, perhaps, the sphinx lamp on the table by the kitchen door, which echoes the Egyptian theme on the portico.

2026 California. Office. Colorist Foster Meagher, who worked with Bert Franklin before starting Color Control, commissioned a local artist to create the Egyptian fireplace mural. A locally designed wallpaper from Winfield Design Associates frames the fireplace.

1807 Octavia between Pine and California. 1876. Italianate. Owner John Blauer and Winfield designer Tom Roberts chose a blue palette for the exterior because Ellen Blauer likes blue. The architectural highlights include the quoins, bracketed major and minor cornices, and the balustrade above the portico.

1807 Octavia. Front parlor. The chandelier and pier glass both came with the house. John Blauer's grandmother taught English and one of her Chinese students gave her the matching étagères that display early 1800s Imari ware.

Besides standing for Blauer, the "B" on the Alaskan marble fireplace (one of seven in the house) stands for the original owner, Charles Behlow, a vice president of H. Liebes, a San Francisco store specializing in furs.

The dried flowers in the decorative fireplace are a Victorian tradition, as are the irises Tom Roberts painted on the walls. A nineteenth-century German clock is the centerpiece on the mantel.

Inside the dome on the coffee table, Queen Victoria is serving tea to Jennie Jerome Churchill. The figures were created by English doll artist Ann Parker. Portraits of Queen Victoria and her consort, Prince Albert, in Victorian frames adorn the fireplace.

1807 Octavia. Stairwell. Because the house was built in 1876, the year of America's Centennial, the sun shines through red, white, and blue glass. The glass is original and the colors change with the sun's movements. The Blauers bought the house in 1976, the country's Bicentennial. Note the Victorian fans and hair wreaths on the wall, and the Polish casket ornaments framing the mirror.

1807 Octavia. *Drawing Room 1880*. The Blauers, owners of The Miniature Mart, have created more than 200 miniature rooms for private collectors and museums. They specialize in rooms of periods they are interested in, and their home is a museum of 25 miniature rooms. They have also created 42 small rooms in a spectacular castle called Maynard Manor, with 8,000 pieces in it.

The rug in this miniature 1880s drawing room is a copy of a Victorian chenille rug in London's Victoria and Albert Museum. It took the Blauers 800 hours to finish its 212 square inches at 2,500 stitches per square inch.

The miniature copy of the William Wooten Patent Desk cost the Blauers more than the original 1874 desk. The laminated rosewood furniture is copied from the work of John Henry Belter.

Ellen made the lamps and dinnerware, the chandelier, carpet, harp, and music stand; John made the architectural enhancements and the chess set. Eugene Kubjack, a famous miniature artist, created the tea set. The candied apples with whipped cream look good enough to eat.

DRAWING ROOM 1880
BY
JOHN M. BLAUER & ELLEN K. BLAUER

221 B BAKER STREET
BY
JOHN M. BLAUER & ELLEN K. BLAUER
1969

1807 Octavia. *221B Baker Street* (famous as the London home of Sherlock Holmes). Since 1965, the Blauers have made eighteen of these rooms, including one for author Irving Wallace. Each one takes three weeks to make. The room is designed according to Bainbridge's Law of Dynamic Symmetry, so that instead of moving from left to right, the eye takes in the whole setting. Some of the books have printing in them, including, of course, *The Adventures of Sherlock Holmes.*

1801 Laguna at the corner of Bush. 1884. San Francisco Stick. Detail. The medium blue body color in this striking scheme is an effective foil for lovely details picked out in cream, pale yellow, white, burgundy, and clay.

1814–28 Bush between Laguna and Octavia. These Italianate row houses with octagonal bays and Stick entrances were built in the early 1870s by Thomas Martin. Just as they did in *Painted Ladies*, the new color designs harmonize well with each other and the neighborhood.

2011–13 Pine between Laguna and Buchanan. 1889. San Francisco Stick. Built by William Hinkel as part of a row of three houses, this classic home was dressed in yellow and white, with ochre-and-blue highlights, for *Painted Ladies*. New owners have transformed it with eighties shades of teal, blues, and grays.

2107–09 Pine between Buchanan and Webster. 1890. San Francisco Stick. Bob Buckter took his color cues from the stained-glass window and dressed up this Lady in pale red, brandywine, three taupes, dark blue-gray, and gold leaf. The unusual swirled columns are artfully picked out in gold and burgundy. In 1978, the doors were the most colorful portals in *Painted Ladies*. Now they have been returned to a chaste natural finish.

2273–75 Pine between Webster and Fillmore. 1881. Italianate. Designer Butch Kardum chose two blues, apricot, creamy white, and burgundy-brown to illuminate the pierced wood balustrade, incised panels, paneled frieze, and the unusual angled doorway of this row house.

Bush Street House. Bedroom. The eleven Bradbury & Bradbury wallpaper patterns in this room are in soft, restful colors that blend harmoniously. The 1840 mahogany four-poster is a family heirloom, as is the 1917 portrait on the wall. The ceiling brackets sporting cupids are original. A nineteenth-century Chinese shawl is used as a top bedspread. A rare nineteenth-century painted leather traveling trunk is used for storage.

(Opposite). Bush Street House. Dining room. When new owners bought this 1882 Italianate in 1984, they found Hippie slogans such as "Make Love, Not War" on the walls in the basement, where the Hippie tabloid *Good Times* was published during the 1960s. Later, the place housed followers of a religious cult.

The great-great-grandmother of one of the owners, Nancy Pope Stockton, came to California from Virginia in the 1830s. Her grandmother traveled the world collecting, and many of her treasures enhance this dining room. The owner spent a year in Japan with her family when she was ten, and she has been collecting Japanese art since then. Her Ph.D. dissertation on East Indian art will focus on Hindu and Buddhist sculpture.

This inviting room combines Federal furnishings with Japanese china of the Meiji period (1868–1912). The fireplace tiles are original. The sun-kissed yellow paint, hand-mixed by the owner, reminds us of Claude Monet's home at Giverny.

2128–30A Sutter between Steiner and Pierce. 1884. Stick/ Queen Anne. Robert Dufort of Magic Brush provided the restoration and the burgundy, blues, grays, and cream color scheme for the if-we've-got-it-let's-use-it architecture. The rare colonnettes, architectural friezes, and turret with soaring gables are highlighted with controlled color.

2691 Sacramento between Steiner and Pierce. 1894(W). Queen Anne row house. The owner of this charming home has lived here for thirty-eight years. In 1986, she got tired of the "dead beiges, the dull colors on the block" and wanted new colors. Who can resist the endearing warmth of this blue, white, and yellow design?

2733 California. Detail. The graceful bouquet of incised cutouts on the columns and the wealth of detail make this house a knockout. (The rigors-of-art-department: The light's on because we changed the bulb.)

2733–35 California between Scott and Divisadero. 1886(W). Stick/Eastlake. A striking balance of quiet colors and highly decorative architecture make this an outstanding example of the new generation of Painted Ladies. Bob Buckter chose gray for the body, white for outlining, and then picked out the architectural details in navy, burgundy, and dark gray.

2717 Pacific between Scott and Divisadero. 1891. Queen Anne. This house was designed by William H. Lillie for builder-speculators James and Moses Rountree as part of a group of free-standing, elegant "fine residences." The belvedere in the gabled attic story boasts exceptionally delicate plaster-work in fleur-de-lys, doughnut, and leaf patterns.

When Richard and Evadna Lynn bought the house in 1974, it was a dreary gray, with a bright red door. Research showed that the original body color had been a dark rose-burgundy, much like the color shown here. With suggestions from the owners, Color Quest's Paul Kensinger followed a Victorian tradition in selecting colors inspired by the original stained-glass window in the living room.

Since the building looked like a Victorian in New York or New England, the Lynns wanted an East Coast look and chose a dark trim, rather than the white prevalent in San Francisco. The gold-leaf accents add a sprightly fillip.

(Opposite). 2717 Pacific. Entryway. While the subdued, bejeweled exterior reflects Eastern color design, the interior of the Lynn home reflects the West Coast penchant for Oriental simplicity. Much of the Chinoiserie was found in antiques shops in Shanghai. The Lynns have decorated the house in a historic manner representative of the 1880s and 1890s period of their home. Most of the detailing and woodwork was still intact because the Coleman family had lived in the house from 1901 to 1957, so there was no devastating continual change of ownership.

The intricate spiderwork-fret room divider just needed staining and polishing. The Hamadan Iraqi hand-tied rug, which dates back to between 1880 and 1890, was the inspiration for the entryway's colors and design. The newly laid walnut floor was designed to fit around the rug.

The colors of the pale wallpaper fill and intricately patterned ceiling—put together by Bradbury & Bradbury Design Service—reflect the rug. The dark wallpaper on the stairway was hung just after the earthquake, and although it looks dark in the photograph, the owners plan to give it a gold wash to restore its original bloom.

The scrollwork on the étagère, an excellent period piece, matches the scrollwork on the fireplace. The cinnabar-lacquer vase, holding fuschias, is dated 1862; the red pepper pot on top is dated 1821; and the chrysanthemum vase is from the late 1800s. The light fixture and Chinese-carved elmwood chest with a richly carved apron are also of the period.

(Right). 2717 Pacific. Front parlor. Paul Kensinger used rag-glazing to give a rosy glow to the walls of this gracious room. The fireplace, of rare Cuban mahogany, is one of five in the home, all different and created by the same craftsman.

Framing the fireplace are two nineteenth-century Chinese nobleman's temple boxes. The Lynns learned that the position of the person owning the boxes, which served as chests of drawers, determined the number of dragons on top. The emperor's boxes had five; these have three.

Holding the pink silk flowers on the hearth is an 1890 Chinese lamp fixture. The white vases with black-and-gold markings on the mantelpiece shelves were wedding gifts to Mrs. Lynn's grandparents in 1880.

2717 Pacific. Dining room. The chandelier and fireplace in this tranquil room are original. The wainscoting had been painted black, but the inside of the pocket doors showed that they were originally golden oak. John Seecamp worked for weeks stripping, graining, and staining to bring the woodwork back to its original condition.

The wooden picture rail near the top of the wall, which adds depth and texture to the "Neo-Grec" Bradbury & Bradbury Art Wallpaper, is made of wood and tooled leather. It, too, needed restoration. Paul Kensinger painted the rosette, which came from San Francisco Victoriana.

The sideboard was made of English pollard oak about 1875. The tea service on the right was another wedding present for Mrs. Lynn's grandparents. Another ancestor, Helen Mount, who crossed the Isthmus of Panama in 1850 when she was ten years old, painted the Haviland china table setting.

The sheer curtains, reproductions from J.R. Burrows & Co., Victorian merchant in Boston, were chosen because their Greek motif matches the Greek motif in the wallpaper. The drapes were handmade and they follow the pattern of the original green velvet drapes found in the music room.

(Right). 3026 Washington between Broderick and Baker. 1886(W). San Francisco Stick. Here's a delightful example of how the judicious use of just one color, the light purple, can make a color design pop. Bob Buckter prescribed gray, off-white, yellow, slate blue, light purple, and a touch of gold leaf.

(Opposite). 3008 Clay between Broderick and Baker. 1894. Queen Anne row house. With his Magic Brush, Robert Dufort restored this elegant façade. The house was once a boarding home for retired White Russian naval officers, and this color scheme could have been inspired by their dress whites. The cream tones and lavish use of gold leaf have produced a dazzling light show.

(Below). Pacific Heights Home #2. Back parlor. This 1882 Italianate was built by contractor Henry Hinkel as one of a row of four one-story homes.

When new owners moved into the house on Thanksgiving Day 1961, their goal was to create a country house with nothing formal in design. Their only design rule was to make their home "a visual report on what we saw and what we liked."

The parlor, decorated with treasures from more than twenty countries, is a testament both to their interests and their eclectic approach to interior design. The room's beige palette was chosen to complement a painting by one of the owners that is titled *Ba*, which is the ancient Egyptian word for the spirit of man.

Pacific Heights Home #2. Dining room. A Baccarat crystal chandelier illuminates this intimate dining room. The artistic centerpiece of the room is *Veronica's Veil*, a painting with a religious theme by one of the owners. A seventeenth-century Japanese sculpture of a novice monk and a seventeenth-century Brazilian sculpture of the Virgin Mary on the mantelpiece add to the spiritual serenity of the room.

Pacific Heights Home #2. Kitchen. Antique animal prints frame this nineteenth-century English country hutch, a setting for Porcelaine de Paris china and objets d'art. The Staffordshire clay figures portray nineteenth-century itinerant American preachers, Mr. Sankey and Mr. Moody, who were extremely popular in England. On the left side in front is a nineteenth-century polychrome Viennese bronze statue by Bergman of an Arabian rug dealer. The handsome, washable, mica-studded Winfield wallpaper has a gritty feel to it.

Pacific Heights Home #2. Porch and garden. Victorian knot gardens were small, elaborately designed to remain green all year round. A photograph of a knot garden in Atlanta led to what the owners jokingly refer to as "Versailles West." The twenty-five-square-foot space and their desire to minimize upkeep dictated the design of the garden. Thirteen trained *Pittosporum undulatum* trees surround the English boxwood hedge.

The Tuilleries-style chair near the hedge is for contemplating the wild strawberries bursting through the brick walk. The trained ivy and flowering plants add to the impression of the porch and garden as a bastion of beauty and tranquillity.

(Right). 1509-11 Baker between Bush and Sutter. 1882(W). Queen Anne. A subdued color combination of gray, gray-green, slate, dusty rose, and creamy white spotlights the unusual ornamentation. The use of aggregate cement in the gable, common in upstate New York, is rare in San Francisco.

(Far right). 2814 Pine. Detail. As he did on the house nearby at 2733 California, Bob used white for outlining the structure of the house and the other colors for bringing out the details. If you listen carefully enough, you can hear the gold leaf singing in the sunlight.

2814 Pine between Baker and Broderick. 1886. San Francisco Stick. Owner Nicholas Caputi called Bob Buckter and asked him to create a color scheme that would get him into the next Painted Ladies book. Bob responded with one of the finest designs in the city. He chose seven restrained colors—pale and deep dusty rose, aubergine, off-white, gold leaf, dark blue, and dark gray-green teal—but he has placed them with unerring artistry and harmony. None of the seven colors is loud, yet the use and placement of the colors complement the architecture perfectly and create a superbly balanced color scheme.

THE WESTERN ADDITION

If San Francisco is the Rome of The Colorist Movement, Alamo Square is the Vatican. The Square is the heart of the greatest collection of Painted Ladies and one of the most important collections of Victorian buildings in the world. Although it doesn't have a St. Peter's, it does have an Archbishop's Mansion.

The Alamo Square area, bounded by Webster, Broderick, Oak, and Golden Gate streets, encompasses the crown jewels in the city's museum of Victorian treasures:

• The Westerfeld Mansion, the Archbishop's Mansion, and 1347 McAllister are three of the most architecturally significant buildings in the city.

• The Chateau Tivoli at 1057 Steiner at the corner of Golden Gate, a bed-and-breakfast scheduled to open June 1990, is also one of the finest Victorians in the city as well as being the greatest Painted Lady in the world.

• Postcard Row on Alamo Square must be the most photographed group of Victorians anywhere.

• In 1967, sixteen bright colors made 908 Steiner, the "Psychedelic House," an enduring symbol of the first generation of Painted Ladies. Today, its gray body color and white trim harbor quiet but ingeniously placed colors that make the house a symbol of the new generation.

• The showcase interior of Richard Reutlinger's home at 824 Grove is a High Victorian masterpiece, a glorious treasure trove of Victoriana.

• The 700 block of Broderick is the most colorful concentration of Victorians that we know of. Jill Pilaroscia's finest work, 700 Broderick, graces the cover of this book.

• Doug Butler's home at 1679 McAllister is the most colorful house in town.

• A block away at 1793 McAllister, Paul Kensinger has proven what a fine artist he is by turning his home into a subtle but superb work of art.

The Alamo Square area presents visitors with a staggering amount of extraordinary architecture and color design, and the collection continues to grow. A number of these homes are open either on tours or, because they are B&Bs, or available to rent for special events. For more information, check the guide in the back of the book.

1057 Steiner at Golden Gate. Chateau Tivoli. 1890. Queen Anne/French Revival. William Armitage designed this massive twenty-two-room dwelling for Oregon lumber baron Daniel B. Jackson, who made it grander still by having his architect add the four adjacent party-wall houses to look like a continuation of 1057's façade around the corner along Golden Gate Avenue. You can even read its name, "Seattle Block," on the central gable. Unfortunately, the four houses are no longer painted to match.

The second owner, Ernestine Kraling, owner of the Tivoli Opera House, was followed in 1930 by a Yiddish school, which made it a cultural center for thirty years. By the time psychologist Rodney Karr and his partner Willard A. Gersbach bought it, the place had become a commune and a center for New Age groups. They found it run down and stripped of all interior woodwork and columns.

Russell Epstein took eleven months to restore the exterior, from top to bottom, using color designs by the owners who were inspired by the pink fireplace tiles in the dining room.

Seventeen colors, plus gold leaf, were used on the exterior: frame green, deep river green, frieze pale green, Portland blue, aubergine, raisin brown, light turquoise, dark turquoise, light and dark clay, dusty rose body color, deep rose trim, duval rose, gray, white, moss, and hickory. The owners spent $6,000 on 23-karat gold leaf to give this magnificent building a paint job worthy of its architecture.

The Baroque top frieze, with musical notes and two designs, was stripped and remade on-site. Portions of it had to be built up and replastered. The classical English Adams relief frieze at cornice level had to be stripped, and in many places was restored by making new molds. Acanthus leaves and other decorations were worked on with dental tools.

Much of the relief had to be stripped and resurfaced. Wood trim had to be duplicated. The siding was extremely soft, so special care had to be taken with it. The entire façade had to be hand sanded after torch stripping. Balustrade spindles were removed for stripping.

The new owners rededicated the house in a celebration of the Harmonic Convergence in August 1987. The house is available for rent for special occasions. In June 1990, Chateau Tivoli will become a bed-and-breakfast with six one- and two-bedroom suites decorated with *faux* finishes and Bradbury & Bradbury Art Wallpapers.

As a cultural center, the Tivoli will offer facilities for seminars and meetings and will also provide guests with the opportunity to attend musical and literary events in the grand style of the Victorian salons.

(Above). 1057 Steiner. This overview of the side shows the cresting restored to bring the only patterned shingled roof in San Francisco back into proportion. The cresting was fabricated by Bay Area Ironworks from Rodney Karr's designs and installed by the Barton Construction Company. The double entry and facing have been completely rebuilt, and the fence is new.

(Right and below). 1057 Steiner. Entryway. Aubergine high-gloss latex was used on the front columns, which resemble the columns at the Palace of Knossos on Crete.

49

(Above). 1057 Steiner. Front balcony. This close-up of the balcony facing Golden Gate Avenue shows off the curved balustrade, new finial reproductions, and the harmonious use of many colors.

(Opposite). 1057 Steiner. Front tower. This close-up of the front tower emphasizes the three friezes and new gilt work. The owner chose to immortalize the mythical Perseus in gilt on the chimney, symbolizing the rebuilding of the once-derelict house.

1057 Steiner. Front parlor. The woodwork in the entryway and front two parlors had to be re-created in plaster and new wood. A century ago, Victorians used *faux*-grained plaster because it was cheaper and easier than wood. Redwood was also *faux*-grained and stained, especially for interiors where the look of oak was desired. The Wedgwood frieze echoes the Wedgwood tiling in the dining room. Lincrusta Walton was added and painted to go with the exterior Adamsesque detailing. Lincrusta is a three-dimensional pressed linoleum– or rubberlike wall or ceiling covering that can be purchased in rolls and is still available through catalogs. It can be painted or stained to order.

1347 McAllister between Steiner and Pierce. 1900. French neo-Baroque, designed by architects Dunn & Schroepfer. In 1987, Bob Buckter redid the color design on this splendid building, which appeared in *Painted Ladies* in shades of brown and cream. Russell Epstein handled the restoration and painting.

The plaster gods and mermaids were in sad shape. On one figure, half of the plaster had "bled" down the side of the house. The nose and half the forehead was eaten away, the arm an open wound, the shoulder out of alignment. Epstein found forty-year-old newspapers stuffed into the open arm muscles. The doorway metalwork had to be stripped and restored as well.

1347 McAllister. Doorway. The golden curlicues over the doorway look like a wig framing a ruby worn by m'lady-in-waiting at the French court. Eleven colors imbue this *belle mademoiselle* with elegance.

1451 McAllister between Pierce and Scott. 1889. Stick/Eastlake. The owners painted this brooding house, notable for its false gable, with a somber brown body relieved by blue, mustard, and red. The newel post in the foreground appeared in *Painted Ladies*. The house is one of originally identical twins designed by William Nooser for the John B. Cariteys.

(Opposite). 1198 Fulton at the corner of Scott. 1882. Stick/Italianate towered villa. The Westerfeld Mansion, San Francisco Landmark No. 135, was built by architect Henry Geilfuss for William Westerfeld, a wealthy Market Street baker who died in 1895. His wife and son operated the business until 1906.

His granddaughter, Juanita Westerfeld Benson, has always lived in an Edwardian flat on Pine Street built by her other grandfather, noted composer William Zech. She has helped the new owners of the building with their loving, hands-on restoration. Mrs. Benson shared Westerfeld mementos with us, some of which appear in the photographs.

John Mahoney, a contractor on the St. Francis and Palace Hotels, owned the house from 1896 to 1928 and added the first garage in town for his Stanley Steamer. Mahoney's friend, Guglielmo Marconi, is said to have made early radio transmissions from the tower room.

After Mahoney, White Russians used the house for a community center that included Dark Eyes, a restaurant and nightclub, until World War II, when it became a rooming house. In the sixties, famous residents included Charles Manson, Kenneth Anger, and Ken Kesey, who, with his Calliope Company, is immortalized in "a freaking decayed giant known as The Russian Embassy" by Tom Wolfe in his book *The Electric Kool-Aid Acid Test*. The owners offer tours of 1198 Fulton that recount its extraordinary history.

The exterior restoration and repainting of 1198 Fulton by Robert Dufort and Magic Brush have been featured in both *Daughters of Painted Ladies* and *How to Create Your Own Painted Lady*.

(Opposite). 1198 Fulton. Front parlor. Granddaughter Juanita Benson looks at home in the Westerfeld Mansion. The jewelry she is wearing was worn here by her grandmother. The Rhine wine glasses, Westerfeld wedding presents, flank a bottle of wine, with a drawing of the Westerfeld House on the label. Aunt Walla Westerfeld gave Juanita the Austrian glass vase on the mantel. The pitchers, glass vases, and family portrait on the organ are also family pieces.

The Bradbury & Bradbury Art Wallpapers "Neo Grec" style wall set and ornamental ceilings were designed by Paul Duchscherer and installed by one of the owners. The snazzy crown ornament tops off this outstanding room.

The house has two sets of front doors. Mrs. Benson told us that, in the days before the telephone, when Victorians were "at home," they left their outer doors open. If they were closed, callers were not being received.

(Right). 1198 Fulton. Back parlor. The corkscrew on the marble sidetable is Grandfather Zech's, as is the silver flask, found in the wall of the Pine Street house. Westerfeld china and silver are in the china cabinet, and family Chinoiserie adorns the original mantelpiece. The globe, lower right, opens up to form a bar.

(Below). 1198 Fulton. Master bedroom. High Victorian Renaissance Revival furniture, part of the owners' taxidermy collection (a Victorian tradition), and the leopard-skin rug add an authentic air to this comfortable, masculine bedroom overlooking Alamo Square.

715 Scott between Fulton and Grove. 1898. Colonial Revival. Grandma Halstead built this house for herself and the one next door as a wedding gift for her daughter. The present owners chose the original colors, which were darker, but they were not around when the house was painted, and the painter lightened the colors. The cream, two pinks, and two blues glow in the San Francisco sunlight. And the gold bracelets on the friezes framing the rounded bays help unify the architecture.

722 Steiner. Front parlor. Carpenter-builder Matthew Kavanaugh built this handsome 1892 Queen Anne for himself and the rest of the six houses on Postcard Row on speculation. Slated for demolition in 1975, the house was saved by visionary Mike Shannon. Inside, there are seven stained-glass windows, a stained-glass skylight, and rumors of ghosts.

This Lady is a star in more ways than one. She is one of the few houses in San Francisco that has an agent. The house has appeared in television shows, commercials, and movies, including *Maxie* and *Invasion of the Body Snatchers*, which also featured one of the houses on Postcard Row.

The spare, modern feeling of this eclectic living room is a striking contrast to the exterior's period charm. The chandelier is a working gaslight. The mantelpiece is identical to the one in the Western Addition #1 parlor. In the 1890s, they were available, with cartouche, from stock catalogs. Mike Shannon designed and manufactured the "Country French" brushed stainless steel coffee table in front of the piano.

1000 Fulton at the corner of Steiner. Archbishop's Mansion. 1904. Colonial Revival/Second Empire. A city landmark. Entryway. Built for Patrick Riordan, the Archbishop of San Francisco, by church architect Frank Shea, the mansion has more than 33,000 square feet, making it one of the city's largest houses. The stairwell is illuminated by a 16-foot stained-glass dome.

After the 1906 earthquake, the mansion served as a refugee center, and the basement vault protected important city papers.

In 1980, Jeffrey Ross and Jonathan Shannon, who also own the Spreckels Mansion on Buena Vista West in the Haight, bought a "disaster" and turned it into an elegant fifteen-room hotel with French touches.

The mansion is the only hotel in San Francisco that is a member of Romantik Inns of the World. The rooms are designed to capture the spirit of the Victorian age. For a romantic, evocative theme that suited the building, located six blocks from the opera, the owners decided to name every room for an opera.

In 1984, the Alamo Square Historic District was created by San Francisco's Landmarks Preservation advisory board. The mansion became San Francisco Landmark No. 151. To Shannon, who assisted with research and support for the committee, "One of the biggest rewards of doing the project was that we feel it was very important in helping Alamo Square become recognized as an important historic neighborhood."

Redwood from San Mateo County was used for this gorgeous tribute to the carpenter's art because it was easy to buy and use. The columns were quarter-sawed to give a tiger-stripe effect, and the capitols and bases of the columns were stained darker than the shaft of the column. Inside the hall, you will find a Bechstein grand piano once owned by Nöel Coward and a pier glass once owned by Mary Lincoln.

1000 Fulton. Front parlor. Larry Boyce stenciled and hand painted the ceiling in fifteen colors using a pattern taken from an Aubusson rug. The owners then decoupaged matching ribbons from an old French paper. The gas and electric chandelier and the Belgian mercury pendulum clock on the mantel of the varnished French Renaissance fireplace are of the period.

1000 Fulton. Carmen Suite. The black-and-red floral fabric would please Carmen. The owners wanted to display a Victorian lace bedspread, but it was too delicate for daily use so they turned it into a mantilla, which floats over the French 1850s bed. The mansion's style of decorating has inspired guests to redo their own bedrooms at home.

1000 Fulton. Carmen Suite bathroom. The armoire matches the 1850s bed in the other room and blends beautifully with the carved French screen, also circa 1850 and still bearing its original blue-gray brocade. Behind the screen, the libretto for *Carmen* hangs on the wall next to the convenience. The Venetian chandelier reflects the period of the room. The contemporary placement of the bathtub must fuel fantasies that it takes a vacation to fulfill.

908 Steiner between Fulton and McAllister. 1888. Stick style. Designed by architects Schmidt and Shea for Nels Iverson, dealer in wood and posts. Known as the "Hippie House" or the "Psychedelic House" when it appeared in *Painted Ladies* dressed in sixteen psychedelic colors, this was one of the first inspirations for the city's Painted Ladies.

In the last few years, the house has reverted to an understated design on the exterior. Bill Wilson created a richly colored scheme that incorporates eight colors of blues, grays, whites, and burgundy to show off the Corinthian pillars and bracketed cornice. With its subtlety and sophistication, 908 is now a symbol for the new generation of Painted Ladies.

Western Addition #1. Radio cabinet. This wonderful neo-Adamesque cabinet, built between 1905 and 1920, is a splendid example of its kind. In the early days of radio, elaborate cabinets in antique styles were built to contain the radio mechanisms for elegant homes. Here, a working Westinghouse radio is housed in a bright cabinet decorated with eighteenth-century motifs in the Adam manner and set on a stand carved in the Restoration style of Charles II of England.

(Above). 824 Grove between Webster and Fillmore. Dining room. Richard Reutlinger led the way toward restoring interiors in High Victorian style in San Francisco and, through books, parties, and word of mouth, across the country. He started collecting Victoriana in 1956 and moved from a four-room cottage to a six-room Victorian, quickly filling it.

He bought this house, an 1886 Italianate designed by Henry Geilfuss, architect of the Westerfeld Mansion, in 1965. The house was in such bad shape it took eight months to put the house in enough order for him to be able to camp out in the parlor. Neighbors who were involved in preservation and restoration empathized and brought sandwiches, champagne, and advice. To Reutlinger, the work was worth it because the house boasts a party room as well as space for his thirteen pianos.

In the dining room, the pier glass is the only piece original to the house and retains the only gilding that had not been painted over. The American silver is in a Renaissance Revival pattern. The Eastlake sideboard matches the dining table. The chairs are English Victorian. The candlesticks are pot metal, typically Victorian.

(Opposite). 824 Grove. Turkish parlor. Having a Turkish parlor or smoking room was extremely popular in the Victorian era. Here men could relax and smoke in privacy. They usually donned a smoking jacket and an embroidered smoking cap, which was something like a fez, to prevent their hair and clothes from retaining the smell of tobacco. The fez on the bust is one of several in Reutlinger's collection.

The dark jewel-like colors and abundant use of paisley scarves is in keeping with the period. The horn chair is from the Midwest, the two lamps are Turkish and movie-house Moorish. One lamp is made of a Turkish lamp base with a cricket cage on top.

The Bradbury & Bradbury Art Wallpapers ornamental ceiling was designed by Paul Duchscherer. It represents five years of discussion, and contains elements from five room sets. The frieze is a copy of the one in the 1884 Emelita Cohen House, a Victorian showcase in Oakland.

To obtain the right glow on the embossed Lincrusta, Joni Monnich of Lilyguild, put on the brightest possible Chinese red undercoat, glazed it, varnished it, and then gave it a gold-wax treatment. Queen Victoria, a gift from a friend who did the framing, smiles out over the case of player-piano rolls. The Egyptian fly swatter from a recent trip and the cobra on the side table fit into the exotic decor.

(On previous spread). 824 Grove. Dining room. This view of the dining room emphasizes the wonderful woodwork that came with the house and the double chandeliers. The wallpaper on the lower dado is by Bradbury & Bradbury, colored to match the frieze, a subtle sunflower design reproduced after an original in Château-sur-Mer in Newport, Rhode Island.

The glimpse into the back parlor, next on the restoration agenda, shows one of the player pianos along with some of Reutlinger's 4,000 piano rolls. His grandfather made the little table out of a walnut tree at the family home in Nebraska. The Christmas garlands are authentic. Reutlinger has been working on his home for almost twenty-five years, and it's still a work in progress.

(Opposite). 824 Grove. Master bedroom. The photographs in this room are of the Reutlinger family. After he took upholstery lessons, Reutlinger himself worked on the draperies and valances in this window treatment. He loves to mix old fabrics. The valances are made from other drapes that were pulled down; the drapes are actually old theater curtains; and the tassels were bought in Rome.

Salvaged silk was stretched on plywood panels for the wall panels. Hank Dunlop helped Reutlinger with some of the design work. Using an 1886 pattern book, Larry Boyce did the stenciling on the ceiling; Eric Fainer polychromed the brackets, which are original to the house and had been polychromed a hundred years ago.

The colors for the room were chosen from the 1870s love seat or settee, which is Dick Reutlinger's most cherished possession. Although the upholstery is later than 1871, since the big design is chenille work, it's estimated at not later than the mid-1870s. The love seat has seven different kinds of needlework, and the rare needlework picturing Sir Walter Raleigh and Queen Elizabeth is original, as is the cord looped around the back. Reutlinger followed the love seat as it traveled to different antiques shops for ten years, never being able to afford it. Finally, in 1975, he found it at a warehouse sale and snapped it up. He feels that "sometimes you're just meant to have things."

824 Grove. Girl's bedroom. The use of fishnet to hold family photographs adds a whimsical air to this feminine room. Reutlinger and his friend, Boston Victorian merchant John Burrows, had discovered a photograph of a Victorian teenager's room that looked like this. The spread is an old family piece. The chandelier, once buried under "a million coats" of white paint, was a present. The scallop shells in the headboard, part of the top-quality nineteenth-century walnut and burl-walnut-paneled Grand Rapids furniture, are echoed in the glowing scallop shells in the Bradbury & Bradbury wallpaper, an exact copy of an 1880s American design discovered in a South Dakota farmhouse closet.

824 Grove. Anglo-Japanese bedroom. The three pieces of this *faux* bamboo American bedroom set, dated September 3, 1881, decorated with carved eagle heads with monograms and Eastlake hardware, are extremely rare. Made of honey maple, with bird's-eye maple panels, the work is unusual because of the Aesthetic design in the panels. The matching accent pieces—the collarbox carved with Oriental detailing and the lacquered frame—were found separately, by accident, by a friend. This was the first Bradbury & Bradbury bedroom to be finished, and the papers reflect the Japanese craze of the 1870s and 1880s in England and America. The polychrome treatment of the woodwork is authentic to this period.

(*Above*). Grove Street Home. Dining room. Joe Pecora, the proud owner of this venerable 1893 Italianate, is restoring his home one room a year. The dining room was finished just in time for Christmas. Since Pecora collects antique Christmas ornaments, this was the best time to photograph the new room. The

Santa Claus collection dates to the 1890s, and the German goosefeather Christmas trees are also Victorian.

Joe found the table in an antiques shop in Benicia, where the antiques shops are a browser's delight. The table came from the Spreckels Mansion on Washington Street. The floor lamp was used with a Victorian organ. Note the authentic treatment of the woodwork, polychromed to blend with the Bradbury & Bradbury wallpaper.

(*Left*). 500–02 Divisadero at the corner of Fell. 1889. Queen Anne. Bob Buckter created a peachy-keen color scheme that illuminates this busy corner and accentuates the many curves and architectural details—especially the detailing under the bay—designed by the Newsom Brothers. The pass-through oval on the corner is unusual.

(*Opposite*). 1679 McAllister between Divisadero and Broderick. 1889(W). San Francisco Stick. Owner Doug Butler and painter Scott Todd of Fine Strokes collaborated on this dazzling outburst of sixties' color to create the most colorful house in the city. Scott likes "as many colors as possible" and he went to town with light and medium lavender, light and medium plum, rose, deep purple, grape, burgundy, and aluminum leaf, which looks like silver foil but doesn't tarnish. Unlike most houses, 1679 has very little body but a wealth of trim. So Doug and Scott started by choosing a lavender for the trim and the palette blossomed from there.

The use of silver dollars for decoration follows an old French custom of making molding with edges marked like the edges of coins. This outrageously colorful scheme seemed shocking at first, especially when it had a bright green accent that was finally decided against, but now we love it. It combines a 1960s sensibility for color with a 1980s concern for detail.

1679 McAllister. Detail. *Faux* finish artist Duane Winters did the mahogany *faux* finish on the doors, and finished the columns to look like granite. Duane feels that the house resembles a bejeweled dowager empress dressed for a ball.

This is Doug Butler's fourth building. For him, buying and restoring and renting Victorians is fun, creative, and a service to the community. "This is my way of being humorous and rebellious. I respect the houses and I'm trying to make a fun statement. Fun does not hurt real estate. I admire Bob Buckter, but he's too subtle for me. Color should mean freedom of expression, but most people don't have the confidence to use color. Give me color. I love color. I want to be colorful but marginally tasteful."

(Left). 833 Broderick between McAllister and Golden Gate. 1901(W). Edwardian. Painting contractor Stephan Leffers designed the four blues, pale baby pink, white, and gold paint that make the eagles on this portico fly.

(Opposite). 1793–93½ McAllister between Broderick and Baker. 1901(W). San Francisco Stick. This exquisite building, the home and office of Paul Kensinger of Color Quest, was a wreck when he bought it in 1984. Before Kensinger restored it, the house had suffered water damage and was falling apart. Now, the striking façade, with its unusual corner columns and double overhang, beckons passersby for a closer inspection. Kensinger's favorite palette is ocean blues, greens, and pastels, and, like other colorists, he finds it easier to pick colors for others than for himself. But the subtle colors, rich design, large palette, and three *faux* marble finishes make this beautifully bedecked damsel one of the fairest of the new generation of Painted Ladies. Paul mixes all of his colors, and for this house they include white, tan-gray, four greens, black, dark blue, maroon, gold, and gold leaf. He put the owl up to protect the house.

Paul Kensinger has been painting since he was eight. He keeps a visual journal of colorful abstract drawings for his daughter, Elysha, along with reflections on what inspires them on the reverse side.

1793–93½ McAllister. Detail. This inviting entrance, finished just before we photographed it, is notable for the three marbleized finishes and for the three cutouts that Paul thinks are the builder's signature. None of them looks Victorian, especially the crosshatching on the pillars and the martini glasses. Kensinger's brother, Mike, designed the stained glass above the doors. The black columns have a purple undercoat, the effect of which is muted by a coat of yellow varnish.

626–28 Baker between McAllister and Fulton. 1893(W). San Francisco Stick. The careful use of color gives this sweet little cottage pizzazz. Note how the detailing on the fence reflects that on the house. The purple body color seen on the house in *Painted Ladies* has now become a warm French blue.

1426 Fulton between Broderick and Baker. 1890. Queen Anne row house. When Jo Shaffer and Clarence Esters purchased this home in 1974, they bought a condemned shingled house that had to be gutted to turn the four terrible apartments into a single-family home.

The façade was redesigned and reconstructed to allow windows to light the third floor (not a practice we endorse).

Bruce Nelson of Local Color received First Place, 1988, in the National Paint & Coatings Association's "Picture-It-Painted-Professionally" contest for his superior restoration work and paint job. Jo worked with Bob Buckter in choosing her favorite colors: mauve, beige, aubergine, French blue, dark green, white, and lots of gold leaf. Since the house has a southern exposure, fading was a prime consideration in choosing a light body color.

Broderick Row. The fourteen Queen Annes on Broderick Street between McAllister and Fulton are the most colorful collection of old Vics in the city. They were built by developers Cranston & Keenan in 1895. Doug Butler spearheaded the drive to get the famous row around the corner from his house painted, sometimes lending money for the job. Bob Buckter did six of the color schemes.

700 Broderick at the corner of Fulton. Three cheers to Jill Pilaroscia for giving this beauty the color design of a lifetime. The owners wanted a happy look. The other side of the street was all cool blues and grays, so they wanted to create a contrast. They loved peach—they already had the terra-cotta balloon shades on the first floor—and the roof of the tower was a prominent green.

Jill, who mixes all her own colors, wanted the siding and shingles to be light for durability. She used what she christened "Lang Peach" (the owner's first name is Lang) on the body; then Leather Pink, named after a Spinneybeck leather sample; and Mary Terra-Cotta, named for the house at 219 Douglass Street, for highlights.

The trim is Shasta white, which has umber in it for durability. Scobel Green (the owner's last name) was used on the bands and picked up in the Broderick Teal window sash. Jill wanted a dark teal accent on the ¾-inch stop surrounding the window. She kept it to such a small area to lessen the effects of weathering.

In addition to the house's wealth of architectural detailing, the pride of 700 Broderick is the massive decorated chimney. It was too lovely to blank out in one color, so Jill chose a *faux* finish in an Argyle sock pattern to go along with the dancing diagonal. She used a glazed finish in pale aqua, a paler version of Scobel Green and Broderick Teal with lots of white in it. Since the color was related, the effect was softer. Color from the building was used for the urn and bouquet. Twenty-three-karat gold leaf makes the trim sparkle.

After experimenting with teal and terra-cotta for the bulkhead, Jill chose another color, a stone taupe. The effect wasn't too busy. It grounded the building and gave a masculine balance to the feminine building. Like Jill's other work and Jill herself, this sun-drenched, reigning beauty exemplifies the Ladies of the eighties.

701 Broderick. This house was owned by contractor Doug Butler, the force behind its new look. Bob Buckter chose four shades of blue, three raspberries, and cream, and Butler added burgundy and more blue.

708 Broderick. Four shades of honey and cinnamon, gray, cream, and navy give this row house the spice of life.

710 Broderick. The owner of this elegant structure wanted an electric house. Bob Buckter supplied it with three blues, cream, and burgundy. Pop goes the building!

1716–18 Fell between Masonic and Ashbury. 1896(W). Queen Anne. Three crisp grays, dusty rose, sparkling white, and a lavish use of gold leaf make this sophisticated Lady sing out. Bob Buckter served as color designer, and Gustavo Caldavelli and his Cal Crew carried it out to a fare-thee-well.

Western Addition House #2. Front parlor. Ron and Anne Smith have lavished love and attention worthy of a queen on their 1893 Queen Anne. The entranceway is graced by three pieces of stained glass by Steven Stevens. A fine collection of Russian lacquer eggs and boxes is in the forefront of this excellent example of a Victorian living room. Also on the table is a Victorian parlor photo album with gilded glass inserts.

The Italian bentwood rocker, dating from the early 1900s, is part of a collection of rockers. The overmantel, which matches the mantel, was found after the Smiths bought the house. Light from a 1920s lamp in the left corner shines on a table holding family portraits framed in silver and pewter. The walls and wallpaper border are green to harmonize with the rug.

Western Addition House #2. Dining room. This warm, inviting room is in burgundy, one of Ron Smith's favorite colors. The ceiling paper border, *Plume* by Schumacher, picks up the color of the fireplace tiles and reflects the brushed-silver ceiling. The sideboard holds a Victorian tea set, part of the Smiths' collection of silver and glassware decanters, and Anne's collection of Wedgwood china. The ceramic fruit centerpiece is Capodimonte. The organ lamp, center rear, is adjustable. Note the unusual fireplace tiles and the ornate initialed silver coal scuttle on the hearth.

Western Addition House #2. Room detail. This turn-of-the-century oak screen, found at the San Mateo antiques show, has three different patterns of Lincrusta Walton. With its hidden hinging, the screen is a stellar example of Victorian craftsmanship.

Western Addition House #3. Parlor. When Tony Inson and Alan Hicklin moved into this small but well-designed 1875 Italianate, which had been relocated from around the corner in 1923, they added urns and an 1820s William IV lantern from a Savannah mansion to the entrance.

Inside, they created an eighteenth-century parlor. The sofa is English, 1790; the Chippendale table dates to 1740; the chairs are Regency; and the serene painting is a 1710 portrait by Sir Godfrey Kneller. The portrait of the woman in the Greek style is in keeping with the period.

Western Addition House #3. Dining room. The bull's-eye mirror, 1800–1810, in this gracious Federal dining room is the owners' favorite piece. The chest used as a sideboard is 1840 French Chinoiserie. The Samson plates are eighteenth century and the Chin Lung Phoenix birds on the chest are dynastic pieces dating back to 1790.

390 Page. Front parlor. Artist William Gatewood and his brother, Beau, moved into a VOV (vacant, open, and vandalized) 1875 Italianate dwelling and are turning the whole building into a work of art. They remember having to chase away people who wanted to be "fellow squatters" just after they moved in. They laugh about the story stating that right after the 1906 earthquake the huge house next door was exchanged for a bag of gold by someone fleeing the city. Thanks to pioneering souls like the Gatewoods, the neighborhood is on the upswing.

The front parlors are elegant in their simplicity. A marble fireplace, examples of Gatewood's art—in this case kimono screens—and an impressive chandelier dominate the space. Gold leaf accents the architectural trim. The Renaissance Revival–style ceiling treatment is original.

Russell Epstein was to begin restoring and repainting the exterior as we were putting the book to bed, and judging from the interior, the house will be worth a detour.

(Opposite). 390 Page. Meditation room. Larry Boyce and his crew of three artists used twenty-three stencils of Pompeiian figures in Victorian patterns and worked six weeks on the ceiling and panel frames of this magical room dedicated to the feminine, the Virgin Mary, and Buddha. The wall panels and screens are paintings by William Gatewood. Beau's wife created the stained-glass windows and the room was blessed by Beau, a former Jesuit priest.

(Right). 198 Haight at Laguna. 1883. Italianate with mansard roof. Thomas Welch McMorey, a real estate speculator and self-proclaimed capitalist, built this house for himself. It remained in his family until 1983 and was purchased completely intact, including the furnishings and the adjacent carriage house.

The new owners have installed a pull-chain convenience, once used in the commode on the back porch, in a new powder room. They love the green body color, discovered on a Sacramento Street house, and Nelson Wolfe of Windsong painting suggested the trim colors.

584 Page between Webster and Fillmore. 1894. Queen Anne. The stained glass by Oakland artist Peter Zajda makes the wisteria that blooms in the front yard in spring blossom all year round. The floor tiles, popular in San Francisco, influenced the color choices of the owners, who worked with Bob Buckter: oyster white, teal, aubergine, warm brown, gray taupe, grape, and the signature gold leaf on the dots. They created a sparkling pearl-and-gold-leaf necklace worthy of a Painted Lady. John Seecamp restored the wood graining on the redwood doors.

(Opposite and above). 415 Fillmore between Page and Oak. 1896–1899. Queen Anne. Choosing the colors for this majestic building was a long process. With the help of persevering colorist Jill Pilaroscia, the owners spent two months swatching to find just the right combination of southwest colors: two tones of raspberry, wine, two tones of blue, cream, and an extravagant splash of gold leaf.

The building's many curved elements give it a soft, feminine quality which is enhanced by the delicate scheme. The gold leaf sparkles in the late-morning sunshine. The wrought-iron fence was painted black to emphasize the house.

815 Page between Pierce and Scott. 1890. Italianate with rounded bays. Bob Buckter worked with the owner of this quiet beauty, choosing dark gray-green teal, dark and bright blue, cinnamon, red mahogany, chocolate, dark cream, dark brown, and cream. Note the ripple effect on the ribbons around the torches on the bay.

865 and 871 Page between Pierce and Scott. 1920 Art Deco Moorish and neo-Victorian. We couldn't resist including this astonishing Deco building, once a phone-company exchange station, then a Masonic hall. Bob Buckter worked with the owner, builder Joe Cassidy, to choose a medium brown body color to enhance the decoration in aubergine, olive gray, raspberry, yellow, navy, and off-white, with gold leaf.

Buckter also created the architectural trim on this house and on the yellow "neo" that Cassidy built next door at 865 Page in 1988. The added gingerbread helps the new structure to fit into the neighborhood. Bob's design blends beige, cream, wine, and navy.

HAIGHT ASHBURY

The Haight is a unique San Francisco mix of the old, the not-so-old, and the new. What's old is a splendid collection of Victorians and Edwardians in any direction you aim.

What's not-so-old is the hippie contingent recalling the halcyon "Hashbury" days of "flower power" and free rock concerts in the Panhandle—that wide strip of greenery bordered by Fell and Oak streets, originally the carriage entrance, that forms a handle for Golden Gate Park. (As it was in the sixties, the word *panhandle* is also a verb.) Joining the remaining hippies on the streets are their successors, members of the New Wave generation out in full regalia.

Another remnant from another era: more used-clothing stores on Haight Street than in any other six-block stretch in town.

What's new is that the Haight's residents have become so upwardly mobile that, despite community opposition, chain stores such as The Gap are becoming attracted to the area. Haight Street includes shops, restaurants, galleries, bookstores (Gary Frank's Booksmith, at 1644, is excellent), and lots of local color, making it one of the most enjoyable walks in the city.

The Haight Ashbury, which includes Ashbury Heights, is bounded by Divisadero/Castro, Fulton, Stanyan, and 17th streets.

1080 Haight at the corner of Baker. The Spencer House. 1885–1890. Queen Anne. German architect Fred T. Ravin designed this imposing structure, notable for its five-sided tower with Palladian windows, for Dr. John C. Spencer.

When Barbara and Jack Chambers rescued the building from an uncertain future in 1984, they asked designer Jill Pilaroscia to change the color scheme that appeared in *Painted Ladies* to a design that would be right for their genteel bed-and-breakfast inn.

1080 Haight. Dining room. When it was built, the back wall of this dining room held a huge, built-in aquarium. By the time the Chamberses arrived, the room was a shambles, and they were lucky to find an eighteenth-century French armoire to hide the problem.

The oak paneling, the sideboard arches echoing the Palladian entrance, and the fabulous original Lincrusta Walton wall covering with silver and gold relief simply needed cleaning and polishing.

Stencil master Larry Boyce spruced up the cake-icing ceiling. The candlesticks and Corinthian-columned lamp were found in London's Silver Vaults. The wonderful vaseline-glass lamps are used for both gas and electricity. The bust of Napoleon is part of a growing collection of Napoleona. Note the beautifully refinished inlaid parquet floors.

1080 Haight. Kitchen. Bradbury & Bradbury irises provide a colorful backdrop for the Chamberses' collection of Villedieu les Poeles copper pots, which Barbara imports and sells. An 1889 iron rack for the San Francisco Meat Company also holds antique chocolate forms and muffin and bread molds. The 1920s hearts-and-stars waffle irons and the turn-of-the-century stove, a Wolf Junior, still make delicious breakfasts.

1080 Haight. Bedroom. The romantic Country French bedroom is Barbara Chambers's favorite, and a real success story. The bedroom set cost $1,000. The flowers, ribbons, and cupids carved on the headboard and footboard were just lumps, hidden under ten coats of white paint. It took three months to strip it all off. Then the images were lightly colored and waxed.

The cupids in the headboard match the cupids in the chandelier, which was bought at an auction for less than it cost to restore and it came from Sally Stanford's house in San Francisco. By accident, the flowers on the lamps match the flowers on the armoire. The feather mattress and embroidered pillowcases are antiques. Barbara found the glazed wallpaper, fabric, and draperies in London.

1283 Page between Baker and Lyon. 1883. Italianate. The house was moved to this lot after a fire in 1893. In the late 1960s, sculptor Sherry Cavan asked Jane Ford to paint a mural on her garage door. To celebrate her twenty-fifth anniversary in the house—"my longest sustained relationship"—Sherry asked Tony Canaletich of San Francisco Renaissance to use her favorite colors for a new design. She loves the positive feeling the house evokes.

459 Ashbury between Page and Oak. 1893. Queen Anne. In 1986, this proud example of Cranston & Keenan handiwork around the corner from 1544 Page was sadly run-down. The owner wanted something to make a statement, something really showy, and he worked with Bruce Nelson of Local Color to restore and paint, from the new garage to the whale weather vane.

BB Color was brought in to interpret the owners' desires in color. Buckter and the owners chose Yacht Basin cream for the body of the house, and accented with bold white, aubergine, ultra teal, and ultra purple. New plaster decorations and detailing were added to the façade. The owner designed many of the plaster figurines that embellish the wall overhangs and front gable. Gold leaf emblazoned on the front gable and wall overhangs complete the impressive restoration. For its work, Local Color was awarded first place in the 1987 "Picture-It-Painted-Professionally" contest sponsored by the National Paint & Coatings Association and the Paint and Decorating Contractors of America.

1544 Page between Masonic and Ashbury. 1891. Queen Anne tower. Although you can't see the sun faces that builders Cranston & Keenan put on the second story, this close-up does show the care they put into their architectural embellishments. This house is one of the many that Cranston & Keenan built in clusters.

(Above). 500–06 Cole at Page. 1890. Queen Anne. The tower on this unique home is in the middle, flanked by imposing gables. The cloverleaf archway in front suggests the "Moorish" influence popular in the 1890s. Bob Buckter had worked with the owners before, and this time they simply told him to "do his own thing." The result is a full range of Buckter gray/blue/green/teals. Some are dark, some are light, some are more blue or more green or true teal. The colors work well together with the off-white and ultra black accents to do justice to this outstanding building.

(Left). 1677–81 Haight between Belvedere and Cole. 1905. Classic Revival. European Painting created a smashing combination of four blues, gray, and white with marbleized colonnettes and rings in the lions' mouths. The style on the façade is rare in the city.

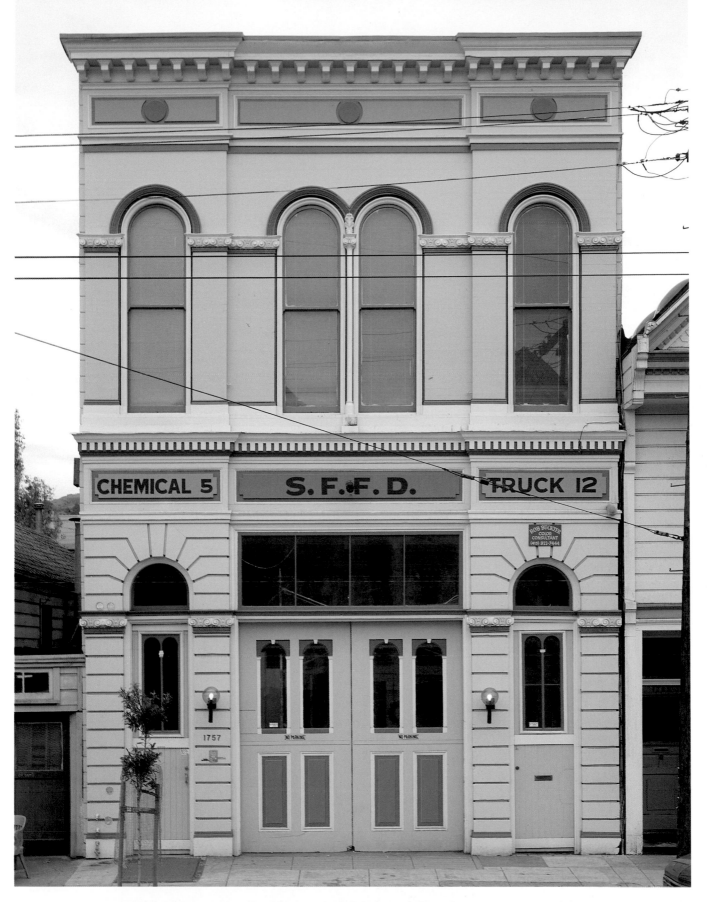

1757 Waller between Shrader and Stanyan. 1896. Italianate. Hose Company No. 30 used this building as a firehouse until 1959. But once again, this handsome Italianate is in the service of the city as the San Francisco Child Abuse Center, providing counseling and a hotline. This paint job was a community project. Armstrong donated the paint and Bob Buckter donated the color scheme of light and dark salmon, burgundy, off-white, and olive gray.

721 Cole between Waller and Beulah. 1895. Queen Anne row house. In *Painted Ladies*, this house was dazzling in sunny golds and oranges. Now she's a lacy Lady in three blue-grays and white with burgundy accents.

357 Frederick between Belvedere and Cole. Queen Anne row house. Muralist Carlos Marchiori "wanted to put the house on a May pole so people could find me." He believes that "people like to glorify familiar symbols." So instead of hanging out a shingle so people could find him, he painted his shingles. And since people like cats, he painted a larger-than-life tiger.

Marchiori specializes in period art interpretations in any artistic style. He paints murals for private homes, hotels, casinos, and department stores, such as the circular ceiling fresco in the Nordstrom's downtown. Artistically, he speaks the dialect of Tiepolo and Veronese, because like them, he comes from Venice. But he never copies; he interprets.

357 Frederick. The Pompeii Room. Marchiori always wanted to convince a client that a Pompeiian room would make a memorable dining room, so he did this as a spare bedroom in the early 1980s. Besides visiting Pompeii and Herculaneum for inspiration, Marchiori was also influenced by the Etruscan decorative style that was popular during the era of eighteenth-century neoclassicism. Marchiori made his own images in a *trompe l'oeil* Roman fresco style.

Marchiori wanted to make the room look as old as possible. He used ordinary housepaint and rolled pieces of paper with white paint along the wall to achieve the look and feel of wear and tear.

Parts of the mural are painted gray to suggest mold. Chunks are blocked out and scraped off. Distressing the paint by rubbing it down with sandpaper also added patina. The room reflects Marchiori's desire for space, which is more important to him than filling a room with furniture and objects. This may be heresy for Victorian buffs, but his sense of whimsy more than makes up for it.

(Above left). 772 Ashbury between Waller and Frederick. 1889. Queen Anne row house. The lumberman who built this house added a final dollop of corn and flowers on the pediment. In *Painted Ladies*, the embellishments were in chaste blue and cream. But the owners' son, Aaron Sanders, chose nine colors—red, dark blue, purple, four greens, white, and light orange to create striking costume jewelry for this Painted Lady.

(Below left). 159 Delmar between Frederick and Piedmont. 1890. Queen Anne. Flowering Japanese cherry trees make a romantic setting for this dollhouse in blues and browns, restored in 1977 by San Francisco Victoriana. The unique witch's hat is completely new, created by architectural restoration designer Stephen Rynerson. An earlier remodeling had added a second story to the building. Paul Kensinger did the color design.

(Opposite). 1315 Waller between Masonic and Ashbury. 1896. Queen Anne row house. This lovely home is one of four Queen Annes built by R. D. Cranston, Senator Alan Cranston's grandfather. After David and Virginia Keller chose their colors, they realized that color chips don't look the same when they are placed on the side of a house, so they worked with Bob Buckter who "put their colors all together."

Authentic period touches include a French porch light and the original handmade lace curtain on the front door. Each house in the group of four represents a different season. With its snowflake decoration, this one is "winter." Next door, the owner of "summer" is taking the stucco off his house, and in neighborly fashion, Mr. Keller is carving the architectural details for him to use in the restoration.

98

(Opposite). 1232 Masonic Avenue between Haight and Waller. 1896–1897. Queen Anne. Built as part of a row by contractors Cranston & Keenan, this home looks like a sister to 459 Ashbury, especially after its four-year renovation and paint job by Brian Moloney and Pago Painting, who went on to paint most of the block.

After the asbestos shingles were removed, woodworkers made new gingerbread. (The initials *S.F.* in the central panel are a modern addition to the Cranston & Keenan trademarks of crosses and Greek keys.)

The owner wanted a blue house. He worked with Moloney to choose Wyoming Dusk for the body, dark blue for shading, medium and light blue, cream as the highlighter, and, Brian's idea, rose for contrast. This endearing, irresistible design is one of our favorites. It's a valentine to a sweetheart that must have been a labor of love.

(Right). 737 Buena Vista West between Central and Frederick. The Spreckels Mansion Bed & Breakfast Inn. 1897. Colonial Revival. Edward J. Vogel built this imposing mansion for Richard Spreckels on what was then rolling empty hills an hour's carriage ride from downtown San Francisco. The original marble wash basin, still at the rear of the first floor hall, was handy for dusty travelers.

During the days of "flower power," a Grateful Dead producer turned the ballroom at the top of the house into a recording studio and recorded the band's early albums there. After a trip to Tibet, the producer's wife worked with Bob Buckter & Friends choosing the colors of a Tibetan temple for her temple of music.

The Spreckels Mansion Guest Suite. In 1979, Jonathan Shannon and Jeffrey Ross, owners of the Archbishop's Mansion, saved this building from being torn down and replaced by condominiums. The interior has been restored and refurbished. Writers Ambrose Bierce and Jack London had studios on the top floor.

Today, the ballroom and two adjoining bedrooms form a luxurious suite that combines a contemporary San Francisco feeling with an Oriental flavor. Antique *obis* (sashes for kimonos) on antique *tansu* chests blend successfully with the modern Japanese wedding kimonos, a contemporary Japanese poster, an old Indonesian puppet, and the classic Burmese standing Buddha.

In the turn-of-the-century ballroom, there were two balconies, one for the band and one for the dowagers. Today, one balcony (seen in the back of the photograph) serves as a sitting area, and the other, behind the newly installed fireplace, is the dining area. Both balconies have spectacular views of the city.

NOE VALLEY & EUREKA VALLEY

This area encompasses four sections. The "Castro," the Eureka Valley section that takes in the area around Castro and Market, is the heart of the city's gay community. Over the past few years, this vital area has seen an influx of new residents. The residential mix of this vital area has become more varied.

Like the Castro, the center of the Noe Valley is a lively, low-scale neighborhood. But it's quieter, family oriented, and host to many of the city's young professionals. Strolling up Noe Valley's main street—24th Street—stopping for an espresso, and browsing in Nicky Salan's Cover to Cover bookstore at 3910 is one of the pleasantest ways the city offers to spend an afternoon.

This whole part of town is worth exploring street by street to discover its wealth of architectural treats.

For the purposes of this book, Eureka Valley and Noe Valley are bounded by Duboce, Dolores, 30th, and Douglass streets. (The house at 32 Caselli is just outside of this boundary off Douglass Street.)

On the Castro Hill separating Eureka Valley and Noe Valley are Noe Heights and Dolores Heights, two quiet residential neighborhoods.

14th Street. Front parlor. Imagination, hard work, and caring friends have helped to create a comfortable, distinctive home out of two condemned 1899 San Francisco Stick cottages. When an Episcopal priest retired, he brought more than memories with him.

The fifteenth-century English chest on the right was a gift from a parishioner as was the Eastlake-style chandelier. Over the mantel, the portrait of a close friend who worked with the owner was done by novelist Barnaby Conrad.

The house was originally two units, and after walls were removed, this front parlor gained two fireplaces, which have been scrubbed down to their original carved soapstone and marbleized metal.

Doug Keister captured this room in its full Easter glory.

14th Street. Altar room. Weddings and christenings take place in front of this sixteenth-century Portuguese chest, which has been converted into an altar that casts a nurturing, spiritual glow. In front is a seventeenth-century *prie-dieu*, and to the right is part of the owner's collection of eighteenth-century Russian and Greek icons.

101

15 Henry. Detail. Jill tests her colors on the house. It took a long time for her to swatch this house, and the body color has been immortalized as Henry Street Blue. Note the pearl tiara framing the doorway.

3666 16th Street. Circa 1890. San Francisco Stick. Who could resist this crisp paint job in plum, gray, pink, and white with gleaming gold trim on a sunny day?

15 Henry between Noe and Castro. 1892(W). San Francisco Stick. Jill Pilaroscia used the most beautiful set of original bay-window stained glass that we've seen as her inspiration for this understated but elegant scheme of grayed turquoise, pink, purple, wine, cream, and gold leaf.

321 Castro between Market and State. The Inn on Castro. 1905. Edwardian. Is this a house or a birthday present? Industrial strength blue, pink, and purple help make this happy scheme jump for joy. The Inn offers eclectic European-style rooms and a cozy atmosphere.

49 Hartford between 17th and 18th. 1902–1904. Queen Anne cottage. Popular contractor
Fernando Nelson designed nineteen houses on both sides of Hartford Street. Stained-glass
artists James Raidl and Roy Little used four grays, gold, and white on the exterior, with dark
gray providing depth.

Illuminated by a late Victorian English street lantern, the luminescent stained-glass door
and window steal the show. The front window, ablaze with bougainvillea, is what Roy calls
an "environmental tie-in to pull the outdoors indoors."

49 Hartford. Front parlor. Collectors supreme, Roy and Jim owned Mammy Pleasant's Parlor, an antiques shop, for seven years. Since 1971, they have been collecting silver, pewter, Art Nouveau, Victorian furniture, photo albums, and pillows with ladies' portraits on them. But judging from their house, they didn't so much close their store as move it into their home. Their treasures fill the house with true Victorian profusion.

The couch in this room is dated 1875; the side chairs and slipper stools are from the 1850s. The 1901 Columbia Disc phonograph still works, as do the French and Austrian music boxes. The gold ceiling rosette is original.

The signed French Art Nouveau statues on the mantel are made of spelter, a white metal with a bronze finish. The fire screen is an unusual Victorian needlepoint. Note the Harrison Fisher woman on the pillow on the right, the French Art Nouveau candlestick on the 1890 Victorian marble-top table, and the 1881 French carriage clock on the mantelpiece.

The framed petit point of a lady holding a dove, dated 1850, came from the estate of Fernando Nelson, as did the small 1917 painting of Wyatt Earp. The Victorian slipper stools near the couch date from about 1850, and the iron coffee table in front of the couch is an 1889 Charles Eastlake.

The owners' favorite pieces include the 1895 brass swan holding books on the floor; *Tulipe*, the bronze on the coffee table by French artist A. Nelson; and *Printemps*, the bronze woman holding doves on the stand in the right corner, signed V. Consten.

49 Hartford. Dining room. When designing glass, Roy always chooses the color first, then the flower. For the dining room, Jim and Roy agreed on pink. Roy's trademark is that his designs break with tradition by breaking the border, so that the border doesn't constrict the design and pulls the outdoors in. The background for these windows is textured clear glass from Remy, France.

The statue on the rare Lloydsweave wicker pedestal is a pewter casting used to mold bronzes, and the exquisite statue on the side table is one of several French bronzes by Moreau in the Raidl-Little collection.

The early 1900s hanging lamp is an unusual apple green. On the right, the 1924 Frugé fabric lamp boasts its original fringe and tatting. A turn-of-the-century Christmas Limoges chocolate set rests on the 1880s Belgian sideboard.

On the handmade 1890s French lace tablecloth are an Eastlake Victorian coffeepot from the early 1870s, early 1900s Sheffield candlesticks, and a 1929 Deco vase. Note the Limoges tureen from the early 1900s, and the hand-painted French tea service with violets accented in gold leaf.

49 Hartford. Bedroom. Roy built this special bed around an English turn-of-the-century glass window.

On the bedstand is an original San Francisco policeman's hat with a dated photo of the policeman wearing the hat in 1904 and his badge, number 338. Victoriana lines the footboard: a pewter White Rock girl bust, a powder jar, inkwell, ruby-glass perfume bottles, cupid candlestick and clock, gilt frame, and an oil lamp with an 1850 cranberry shade.

The 1920s articulated armor of filigreed brass was found in a costume shop in Italy. The 1915 bicycle carriage is a child's pedal toy designed like a surrey; the Teddy bear is from the same year, but the sea captain came from a friend. The long box in front is a Victorian glove box. The enlisted man's 1881 helmet is decorated in 24-karat braid.

Bon Soir, the lady of the Moreau lamp, blows a good-night kiss while sitting on a new moon. And the turn-of-the-century Diana, goddess of the moon and the hunt, serenely surveys her domain.

(*Above*). 49 Hartford. The Pub. This Tudor-Jacobean pub is used for parties. Roy constructed the table and the floor from warehouse roofing. In keeping with the spirit of the period, the table has no nails. Gold tones on the walls and ceiling highlight the texture and give an authentic feeling of age.

Roy carved the cigar-store Indian and restored the 1930s carousel animal and the 1920s barber pole. A late 1800s window serves as a room divider. The early 1900s wood stove keeps the pub warm.

The platform rocker dates to the late 1800s. Hanging above it is an 1849 red-and-green well pulley. German mugs, a Sheffield walnut-shaped meat cover, and Friar mugs and china share the table and shelves with Roy and Jim's pewter collection. The painted beer stein is a Roy Little original.

(*Opposite*). Eureka Valley. Kitchen. Richard Wagner is a Renaissance man: an ecologist, former professor, author of a successful textbook, world traveler, artist, and composer. His remarkable 1887 Stick/Eastlake home reflects his interests and artistic gifts. As are most Victorian homes, his has been a work in progress since he bought it in 1974.

Richard regards his home as a personal statement against the disinterest in ornamentation in modern culture. "I need a lot more ornamentation in my life," he says. "Apparently, other people agree because ornament is coming back into style."

To satisfy his need for ornamentation and his preference for curves instead of hard edges, Richard has spent the last fourteen years single-handedly designing and painting every flat surface he can find. Even the doors have been painted to unify what's around them.

Richard also needs to bring nature indoors, and his home is an inspired, delightful blend of nature and artifice. He wanted to make the interior of his home as psychologically warm as possible as a foil to the coolness of San Francisco.

Volcanic colors were chosen to create a sense of warmth. The philodendron forms a magnificent canopy for his intricately painted table. Wagner collects found art, his response to the manufactured art society generates, and he decorated the kitchen with rocks, animal skulls, and other souvenirs of his travels. His collection of pottery also adds a natural feeling to the room.

He designed the fireplace surround, made of particle board, to match the fireplace in the front parlor and then marbleized it.

Eureka Valley. Bedroom and office. Sunshine paints this room all day long. Wagner decorated the clear window sash and created a rainbow effect by surrounding it with colored glass. Painted hummingbirds and butterflies float on the cool, sky-blue ceiling. The onions and shallots on the floor grew in a community garden on Potrero Hill.

Eureka Valley. Music room. The decoration in the other rooms has evolved over time, but the music room was designed as a whole and most of it was painted in a month. Wood surfaces, including the large horizontal speaker against the wall, have been marbleized.

Inspired by the movie *Amadeus*, Richard added silhouettes of Mozart on the ceiling. Except for the piano at which Richard does his composing, the musical instruments were found at flea markets. Note the cherubs on the richly colored rosette. With cherubs and Mozart as your muses, think of the beautiful music you could make in this warm, lovely room.

Eureka Valley. Living room. The centerpiece of the living room is the original marble mantelpiece. Above it lies the barque *Strafford*, which plied the China trade out of New York and was owned by Wagner's great-great-grandfather. The girandoles have been in the family for more than 150 years. Wagner signs his rooms by discreetly integrating his initials into the decorative ruffles and flourishes.

Eureka Valley. Guest room. A remarkable blend of nature and art are in full bloom in this small guest bedroom. To give the illusion of more space, Wagner painted a stone wall to create the fantasy of a magic pavilion looking out onto a wilderness. The mural offers a 360-degree view from the house without the city in the way, Richard's vision of what San Francisco looked like 300 years ago before it was settled. This view looks south at Dolores Heights. A butterfly, condor, and mountain lion are among the fauna that made the area their home. Celtic knot patterns were chosen for the borders because Wagner enjoys the intricacy of their design.

217 Douglass between 18th and Caselli. 1897(W). Queen Anne row house. The first owner of this house, a calligrapher, paid $1,200 for it. The present owner bought a condemned, stripped, asbestos-covered waif. All of the gingerbread is new, re-created by Haas Woodworks. Inspired by the last house on the left on Postcard Row on Alamo Square, they chose gold, light yellow, tan, and rust, which is reflected in the sunburst.

(*Below right*). 219 Douglass between 18th and Caselli. 1893. Stick. Jill Pilaroscia created the scheme for this storybook cottage built for a carriage painter who became a car painter. His son, born in the house, lived here for seventy years. The grace, delicacy, and seductive femininity of this design are enchanting. The choice and the placement of the colors emphasize the jigsaw detailing animating the façade.

(*Below*). 219 Douglass. Detail. The seven colors that Jill Pilaroscia chose to illuminate this panel provide an outstanding example of attention to detail. They turn these simple details into jewels, the perfect finishing touch in the finery of this Painted Lady.

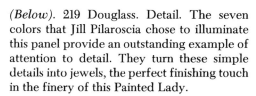

32 Caselli between Douglass and Clover Lane. 1908(W). Queen Anne. For the Painted Lady who has everything Bob Buckter fashioned a brooch fit for a queen. Turquoise, blue, grape, dark green, aubergine, yellow, off-white, and gold leaf bounce off the mauve-taupe body color, and the necklace of gold leaf on wine in the cornice molding brings it all together. This ornamental collage may not be original to the house.

708 Castro between 20th and Liberty. 1883. Stick/Eastlake. Tour buses have been stopping in front of this house, designed by Fernando Nelson, a major builder of the decade, since the block appeared in *Painted Ladies*. Nelson's trademark is the cut-out circle or donut pattern found in the doorway panels and in the decorative strips framing the windows and doorway. In 1985, John Johnson told color designer Paul Kensinger that his favorite color was forest green. Then they worked together to pick five shades of green, white, black, dusty rose, and gold leaf to play around it. The house has a panoramic view of downtown.

712 Castro between 20th and Liberty. 1894. San Francisco Stick. Charles L. Hinkel designed this wide paneled door with its diamond-shaped ornamentation. Then Jill Pilaroscia turned it into the most colorful door in San Francisco. She brought out the Japanese flavor of the detailing with a combination of coral, peach, white, and aubergine.

725 Castro between 20th and Liberty. 1898. Stick/Eastlake. The exquisite balance and harmony between these delicate colors make this one of the most beautiful bay windows in San Francisco. All hail Color Quest's Paul Kensinger for this perfect example of an eighties Lady. Its colors and design are the stuff of poetry, but its subtlety proves once again that a camera is no substitute for a pair of eyes.

727–29 Castro between 20th and Liberty. 1898. Stick/Eastlake. Contractor Fernando Nelson would be quite pleased with the modern color approach to this stately row house. Nelson lived in a Queen Anne tower house at one end of the block, and his brother lived at the other end. One local owner feels that they simply kept building down the block until their houses met in the middle.

In *Painted Ladies*, the house and the one next door were dressed in earth tones. The new outfits are in 1980s colors—three shades of turquoise, raspberry, two shades of burgundy, cream, and a profusion of gold leaf—deftly designed by Paul Kensinger of Color Quest. Paul color-designed four of these homes and found it fun to work with a row of houses. Small wonder this block is on the tour van route.

3833 21st Street between Noe and Castro. 1905. Queen Anne. Three shades of blue-gray, bright and dark blue, and cream make the embellishments on this house, built by contractor John Anderson. The triangular bay with a spiral colonnette is rare. Check out Hill Street between Noe and Castro for other good-looking Victorians.

906 Noe between 22nd and Alvarado. 1905–1906. Queen Anne row house. This flowering Grecian urn is a cool summer bouquet. The relatively unadorned architecture looks as if it had been dipped in sherbet: peach, raspberry, and vanilla with teal and dark teal added for contrast to bring it all together.

Developer Jack Schlotthauer of Foxwell & Company, the real estate investment development firm that owns the building, did the color design on the house, which was part of a tract constructed by builder John Anderson.

(*Opposite*). 1075 Noe between Elizabeth and 24th. 1888. Stick. The sprightly use of pink, blue, and cream to accent the beige body color gives this stately home an innocent, fairy-tale quality. Note the way the brackets extend all the way down through the triple friezes. The owner chose the colors and then painted the house himself in 1979 and again, with the same colors, in 1987. He used wood scaffolding that he built himself.

(*Left*). 1075–77 Noe. Detail. The color and placement of every element of this doorway, including the lace curtains, has been carefully thought out. Since painting the house was a labor of love, the owner took the time to paint the clapboards on the side in the same colors as the rest of the house.

4128 24th Street between Castro and Diamond. 1895. Queen Anne. When realtor B. J. Droubi and fireman Terry Lee moved into this home, lots of work had to be done, starting with the removal of asbestos shingles. Since they were going to do all that work, they went a step further and made it *their* house.

They hired Rick Schaefer to custom design the wood carvings: a fire ax and realtor's *R* at the peak of the gable, fire nozzles squirting water at the lower gable corners, the blackberry brambles of their backyard in the detail of the second-story corner window, as well as three baby birds in a nest representing the couple's three children.

The desert flowers forming the archway above the front steps are a remembrance of Droubi's Arizona childhood. Droubi explains that "the previous owner had taken all the fun out of the building. It's kind of corny, but once you start restoring, you might as well make it personal." Jill Pilaroscia added the finishing touch of "Neapolitan" colors—chocolate, vanilla, and strawberry, with a liberal sprinkling of gold leaf.

(Above). 221 Jersey between Noe and Sanchez. 1891. Stick Cottage. The waffle pediment with its tree-of-life design gives the house panache. Interior designer Cynthia Baron, who found some of Richard Reutlinger's treasures, feels that color is the most important gift you can give your home.

For hers, she wanted light colors, the colors of the calla lilies that bloom in her yard, creamy white and bright stamen yellow. Cynthia says that the robin's-egg blue "makes my heart sing."

(Opposite). 1189 Noe between Jersey and 25th. 1891. Stick/Eastlake. Richard Zillman, who is active in the Victorian Alliance, told Bob Buckter that he wanted to hear the sound of car brakes screeching when people stopped to goggle at his house. His wife, Cher, loves bright yellows and collects carnival animals, and she wanted a circus wagon.

The combination of two yellows, white, brown, red, purple, black, burgundy, and gold leaf is guaranteed to produce a smile. Clark Chelsey of Chelsey Painting experimented for just the right shade of yellow. Cher Zillman did the gold leafing on the façade by herself. Note that alternating top and bottom triangles in the panel of diamonds over the window are painted silver to catch the light.

(Right). 1189 Noe. Door. The Zillmans added a paneled door, newel posts, carved gable ends, stained glass, and other ornamentation to the building.

(Opposite, above). 1566 Sanchez between Valley and 29th. 1889. Italianate. Inspired by her sister, who is an artist, the owner—who knits and does needlepoint and silk dyeing—chose her favorite colors: brick red, yellowy cream, navy trim, orchid, and gold paint. Then Strokes, a company of women painters, did the work.

1238 Church between 24th and Jersey. 1895. Queen Anne row house. On a row house notable for its lap siding and plaster swags, the owner-architect and his wife created "an Easter bonnet for a Painted Lady," while renewing the house at Easter time in delicious Mediterranean colors.

(Opposite, below). 1097 Church at 23rd. 1903. Edwardian. Owners Chez Touchatt and Larell Fineren conspired with color consultant and interior designer Lou Ann Bauer of Bauer Design to have some fun with their house. Lou Ann used black, white, and purple to indulge in a bit of stenciled whimsy: a painted frieze of Popeye's "goil," Olive Oyl, bopping up to 24th Street to pick up a can of spinach. Ron McCambridge of Peacock Painting sent Olive on her way. The rest of the house is painted in two greens, purple, and cream.

Lou Ann's goal is to unfreeze the city's friezes by designing them with animals that have a sense of motion to them. Animal lovers may want to visit her kangaroos at 1504 Sanchez, and rabid rabbit fans may want to take the six-block hop up to 121 Hoffman to see the bunnies on Lou Ann's home. When we spoke to Lou Ann, she was about to face the next challenge in the creation of her urban menagerie: animals for a pet hospital at 2308 Lombard.

THE MISSION DISTRICT, POTRERO HILL, AND THE BAYVIEW DISTRICT

Aglow with spectacular, brilliantly colored murals, the Mission remains the most colorful part of the city. The mural on 24th Street at the corner of South Van Ness Avenue, "Festival de las Americas," captures the spirit of the Mission, of Carnival, and of the annual 24th Street Cultural Festival.

The mural includes portraits of neighborhood people and businesses. If you look carefully, you can see how the artists gave the singer's arm a three-dimensional quality with an artfully placed strip of wood.

The oldest established section of San Francisco, the Mission was born when Fra Junípero Serra founded the Mission Dolores (City Landmark #1) on October 9, 1776, in one of the sunniest parts of town.

The district has retained its Hispanic flavor since that time. The Latin American artists who have brightened the streets are continuing the tradition, which was started by Mexico's finest artists, of painting murals to delight and educate the public.

Café Picaro at 3120 16th Street offers a congenial atmosphere for the Mission's creative souls. Five blocks away at 968 Valencia is Modern Times, the city's leading "politically correct" bookstore.

The Mission district is bounded by Dolores and Highway 101 and by 16th Street and Army.

464 Fair Oaks between 25th and 26th. 1888. San Francisco Stick. Impertinent touches of raspberry, cream, and gold leaf highlight the festooned frieze, the brackets at the cornice, and flattened pediment of this stately Stick built by John Coop. The gilded iron cresting over the entrance is original.

435 Fair Oaks between 25th and 26th. 1888. San Francisco Stick. John Coop also designed this house, and the owner chose three lovely shades of cream and blue to accent the marvelous architectural ornamentation of festoons, eyelet scallops, squeezed pediments, and fluted pilasters. The iron cresting over the portico is a replica of that on 464 Fair Oaks.

1286 Guerrero between 24th and 25th. Circa 1890. Queen Anne. The tan, light green, and white design for this splendid home was picked up from the tiles in the entrance. What the design lacks in contrast, the house makes up for in architecture. The original owner, Christian Hellwig, was an Austrian tanner who chose a tower house to show off his new-found wealth.

1265 Guerrero between 24th and 25th. 1889. San Francisco Stick. Like a spring bouquet, this delicate scheme has two shades of green with lilac flowers and accents. The owner runs Cosmetic Comfort, a center for people recovering from cosmetic surgery, and wanted cheerful, comforting colors on the exterior as well as the interior. Built by architect B. E. Henriksen, this house still has its original false gable and iron fence as well as the cut-glass transom and Ionic colonnette in the entry.

210 San Jose between 24th and 25th. 1878. Italianate. Since 1963, color designer Butch Kardum, the father of the art, has painted this home three different ways. Because he doesn't like to repeat himself, each design he does is original, so he does not do many homes. Now in what he calls his "pastel period," Butch used seven colors this time: three grays, burgundy, off-white, brown, gold paint, and gold leaf.

Mission Home #1. Hallway. The owners of this classic Italianate used mauve and light blue accents on a rice-paper white background in the front rooms. The chandelier is original, as is the walnut-burl newel post with walnut inlay. Bob Haas helped restore the wood carvings and trim in the house. The bracket is a replica of Lorelei done by Agnes Pritchard for San Francisco Victoriana.

The Renaissance Revival hall stand was found at a garage sale. Charles Eastlake once wrote that an étagère should be a miniature museum for a homeowner's treasures, a mandate fulfilled here. The alabaster bust was found on a salvaging job.

Mission Home #1. Garden. Collecting is a Victorian passion. Part of one owner's collection of antique and modern "chickeniana" enlivens this quiet garden, a perfect spot to relax in the middle of the Mission.

200 San Jose at the corner of 24th. 1877. Italianate. Butch Kardum worked with the owner to perfect this striking, jazzy color design.

988–90 Guerrero between 21st and 22nd. 1894. Queen Anne. The owner worked with Robert Dufort of Magic Brush to create a distinctive Painted Lady. She choose feminine gray and light and dark purple—dowager's colors—for what she fondly called her "old ladyish-looking" house. Built by architects McDougall & Son, it combines Moorish details with a wealth of decoration.

Mission Home #2. Stairway. Judge Daniel J. Murphy, whose wife was active in the women's suffrage movement and once hosted Susan B. Anthony, built this Italianate in 1878.

With the help of a friend, the present owners refinished the banister, which is built with glue and wedges and has no nails. The woodwork, which curves as it descends, is a triumph of the woodcarver's art.

The stairway's two coffin niches are framed with *faux* marble surrounds, and illusion paintings of curtains and tropical vistas. After the niches were painted, the owners found two temple jars in a Hong Kong pottery factory. The molding and plasterwork is from San Francisco Victoriana.

Mission Home #2. Living room. Throughout the house, the owners wanted to respect the architectural detail of the building. They also wanted a contemporary but comfortable feeling, a tasteful, welcoming blend of old and new.

The windows, the sunlight, the view of the garden, the light-colored walls and furniture, and the fourteen-foot ceiling all conspire to give this eclectic room an airy, summery feeling.

The simplicity of design draws attention to the 1875 sideboard in the dining area and the pier glass, which was discovered at Butterfield & Butterfield. The china was made in Carlsbad, Austria, and was a gift to one owner's great grandparents, who lived in Stanislaus County. The marble fireplace was made in San Francisco.

Mission Home #2. Bedroom. A five-piece Austrian bedroom set anchors this tranquil nook. Note how the lamp echoes the trumpet-of-Gabriel vine in full bloom on the patio.

3755 20th Street. The Presidential Room. When the earthquake burned down the Danish consulate on Market Street, Consul General Hans Birkholm moved his office into this second-floor room in his home, a handsome, semimansarded 1887 Italianate with a spectacular view of downtown San Francisco. Because he came from a seafaring family, Birkholm enjoyed watching the ships steaming into the bay.

A devoted FDR fan, Jim Lovegren has been collecting presidential memorabilia for twenty-five years. His collection makes this room a colorful museum of American history. Buttons, flags, glasses, and pictures create an aura of exciting times past, of races won and lost.

John Seecamp created the *faux bois* walnut finish on the doors and paneling. The room is patriotically painted flag red, white, and star-spangled blue.

3877 20th Street between Dolores and Church. 1907. Edwardian. Facing Dolores Park and blessed with a postcard view of the city, colorist Bob Buckter's home boasts thirteen colors, including his favorite Ultra Purple and Ultra Green, which no client has been brave enough to let him use.

573 South Van Ness Avenue between 16th and 17th. 1878. Queen Anne. This imposing building, which appeared in *Painted Ladies*, was originally surrounded by expansive grounds. In 1985, the owner, realtor Robert Imhoff, chose a bright brick red as a new accent color to wake up the color scheme of medium and dark brown and ivory.

(Below). 919 South Van Ness between 20th and 21st. 1889. Queen Anne Eclectic. The Flemish gable and unusual Baroque double volute and *l'oeil de boeuf* window set this house apart from any other in the city. The owner of this remarkable edifice, once a rooming house, chose colors he liked, colors that were not elsewhere on the block, and then worked with Bob Buckter on placement.

The scheme of cobalt blue, cream, almond, olive, lilac, maroon, and black had to complement the red roof. This one-of-a-kind house was still being worked on when Doug Keister's sun-kissed photo captured the stark, dramatic, high-contrast color scheme. The paint job was done shortly after the owner moved in because he feels that, "If you make the outside look good, it makes the neighborhood better. Then we can tinker with the inside."

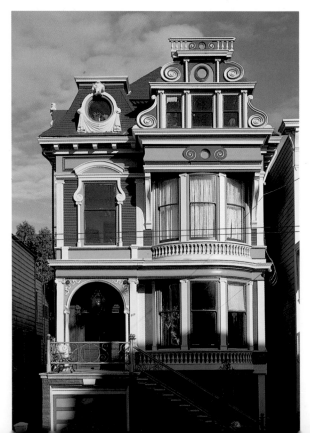

(Above). 825 South Van Ness between 19th and 20th. 1910. Edwardian. BB Color strikes again. Bob Buckter had done a previous house for the owners on Sanchez, and they put themselves in his hands. He came up with a stunning combination of two gray-greens, Brackenhouse gray, oyster white, and burgundy. The finials are new. When looking through a scrapbook on the house, which the owners bought from sons of the original owners, they discovered the house's first phone number: Bush 178.

772–74A Shotwell between 21st and 22nd. 1879. Italianate. With its graceful tiara, this beauty is one of our favorites. It is unique in both color and architecture. Owner Richard Zillman commissioned Butch Kardum to create a fresh, felicitous color scheme of light, medium and dark mauve, burgundy, light and dark blue-gray, aqua, off-white, brown, and gold leaf.

772–74A Shotwell. Detail. Note how Kardum used gold leaf to add sparkle on the leaves in the Corinthian capitals of the columns and how the band of aqua helps make the whole color scheme work.

3171–73 24th Street between Shotwell and South Van Ness. 1886. San Francisco Stick. Before moving to St. Louis, colorist Joe Adamo lived here and painted the building in contrasting Native American colors for the owner, a Native American. The colorful result had the power and impact of a mask worn to keep the house safe from dull colors.

956 York between 21st and 22nd. 1895. Queen Anne cottage. Owners Dave Bezoni and Sid Stafford have been working on this charming little cottage since 1980. The white and light and dark blue scheme is highlighted by the use of gold paint to pick out the veins of the leaves in the gable. The owners definitely turned over a new leaf in color design!

1334 Utah between 24th and 25th. 1895. Stick/Eastlake. This house was built by one of the owners of the half-dozen railway companies that later became the MUNI (MUNIcipal Railway). When it appeared in *Painted Ladies*, it was dressed in dark Wedgwood blue with burnt orange and cream. Its new finery is a combination of nine colors, including blues, greens, white, black, gray, violet, and gold.

The checkerboard sections are like parquet, with three-dimensional lines running across the squares of wood in different directions to heighten the checkerboard effect.

597 Arkansas past 20th Street. 1885. Italianate/Stick. The owners chose light and medium pink, white, gray, and aqua for their deceptively small cottage because they liked the contrast between the warm and cool colors and the way the colors vibrate together. They also feel that the design fits in with the aesthetics of the neighborhood, which is now perking up.

At the end of this row of ten cottages on a quiet street on Potrero Hill, the man who constructed the row built himself a two-story home on a thirty-foot lot by appropriating land from the cottages, making 597's lot only twenty-three feet. They tried to make up the space by planting a garden in front and by adding to the back of the house.

The Italianate at 555 Connecticut that appeared on page 78 in *Painted Ladies* is a block away and still wearing the same cheerful outfit.

1556 Revere between Lane and Keith off 3rd. The Sylvester Mansion. 1865. Italianate. A City Landmark. We saved our most exciting discovery for last. This 8,000-square-foot-home is one of the oldest and finest Victorians in the city. Stephen Piper, builder of the South San Francisco Opera House, spent five years building the Sylvester Mansion for the Sylvester brothers who operated a dairy ranch in the Bayview and Hunter's Point area. In 1911, the house was moved from Quesada, one block north.

When antiques dealer Linda Blacketer discovered it, she decided that she had found her dream house: a big Victorian, in a sunny neighborhood, that needed love and attention. After extensive restoration of the exterior, the house was painted in Confederate gray-blue, and accented in burgundy, navy, cream, and gilt.

To ensure its future preservation, the façade has been deeded to the Foundation for San Francisco's Architectural Heritage. Linda specializes in American Victorian pieces and hosts an open house on the third Saturday of each month.

1556 Revere. Living room. Once a ballroom, this elegant space welcomes visitors with cosy sitting areas, including the Renaissance Revival parlor set in the foreground. The original ornate stenciling on the ceiling has been retouched, and the rococo gold-relief work, with a five-inch-deep cove, has been restored. Linda is particularly fond of the pump organ.

1556 Revere. Living room detail. In 1913, a young Sylvester painted this lovely lady on the wall in what was then the ballroom. The lamp shade is made of fabric reworked from antique shawls.

1556 Revere. Master bedroom. The American Renaissance Revival walnut bed, washstand, and étagère were made around 1860. The French floral wallpaper is by Inaltera. Note the fainting couch, a standard furnishing in a Victorian master bedroom.

1556 Revere. Children's bedroom. A fabulous English corner cabinet glistens in this sunny front room, where Victorian dolls and toys frolic. Note the wicker bird cage holder by the fireplace now freming a plant.

THE LIVING END

Neptune Society Columbarium. 1 Loraine Court off Anza between Stanyan and Almaden Court. The Neptune Society is restoring this marvelous building, designed by B. J. S. Cahill and built in 1898, in a classical Beaux Arts design blending Roman, Baroque, English neoclassicism, and nineteenth-century polychrome in the tradition of the American Renaissance, which sought to regard death without fear or morbid feelings.

Bob Buckter's lovely, tasteful color scheme makes the Columbarium look like the unique architectural monument it is. The Columbarium's historian, Dale Suess, gives tours on Saturdays.

Neptune Society Columbarium. The rotunda. Memorial services are held in the rotunda, which reaches a height of about seventy-five feet. The stained-glass cap below the dome is about twenty-two feet across. The richly designed plaster decorations are deftly picked out in warm blues and browns.

146

Neptune Society Columbarium. "Three Angels in Flight." This sublime stained-glass window, one of six on the first floor, may have been designed by John La Farge. The folds in the angels' garments are rendered in high relief, giving the glass a tactile three-dimensional quality.

Epilogue: A Call to Colors

Do what you can with what you have where you are.
— Theodore Roosevelt

One of the satisfactions in writing the Painted Ladies books is that they give us the opportunity to continue our dialogue with our friends in the Victorian network around the country: the homeowners, colorists, painters, craftspeople, architects, historians, preservationists, city planners, and fans of Victoriana. We hope that this new book will broaden the network to include interior designers. If you have read this far, you are probably in at least one of these groups.

Having a sense of mission about recording The Colorist Movement comes to us easily. These books are a labor of love for us, and we know that they are historical documents whose importance will increase as time goes by.

But the four books about Painted Ladies that have been written up to this point came about not because of us but because of people like yourselves: courageous homeowners, first in San Francisco and then around the country, who made their houses worth capturing for posterity.

This happened spontaneously. No one asked the homeowners to do it. Indeed, they often endured insults for their efforts until their neighbors appreciated what they were doing and started creating their own Painted Ladies. We are all creating The Colorist Movement together as we go, and you know as much as we do about where it will go next.

The Forces of Darkness

But out there, in numbers far greater than the Victorian network, are the forces of darkness, the people who:

- Don't know or don't care about Victorians
- Know and care about Victorians but are afraid to speak out
- Believe that building our future justifies destroying our past
- Don't take care of their Victorians
- Ruin them through ignorance in trying to improve them
- Want to tear down as many Victorians as possible and construct ugly buildings as their contribution to the-biggest-bang-for-the-buck-and-to-hell-with-posterity school of architecture.

You can't calibrate the value of being able to admire and learn from a Victorian. Keeping the forces of darkness at bay requires eternal vigilance and an enlightened, passionate, and mobilized Victorian network. If you own a Victorian or love Victoriana, you are part of the Victorian network.

If you would like to put your passion to good use, here are some suggestions:

Learn about Victorian culture. Read books, attend lectures, take a course, take a trip, subscribe to *The Old-House Journal*, *Victorian Homes*, *Historic Preservation*, *Early American Life*, and *Victoria*.

The more you know, the better able you will be to defend threatened Victorians, to understand your house, and to balance respecting tradition with creating a new one.

See as many Victorians as you can. Life offers few pleasures more satisfying than roaming around San Francisco with Doug Keister on a sunny day shooting pictures of gorgeous buildings.

The houses in this book are laid out in an easy-to-follow pattern, taking one-way streets into consideration. You'll enjoy the Honorable Mention houses too and there are always more homes being done up as Painted Ladies. Start a photo collection of your own.

But wherever you live, we urge you to visit Victorians. Outstanding Victorians that are private homes, B&Bs, museums, offices, and restaurants are liberally sprinkled across the country. Visit them to appreciate the different approaches to color, architecture, and interior design. You will find ideas that will help you with your home.

Develop your Victorian network. Join local preservation groups and national organizations such as the Victorian Society of America based in Philadelphia (East Washington Square, 19106; 215-627-4252) and the National Trust for Historic Preservation based in Washington, D.C. (1785 Massachusetts Avenue, 20036; 202-673-4000).

Give a Talk. We've been called evangelists preaching the gospel of color. When you know enough to give a slide lecture, why don't you start converting the unenlightened? Almost every town has groups that meet once a month and need speakers. Go forth and spread the word about the value of Victorians and the importance of preserving them.

Adopt a House. Wouldn't it be wonderful if every town in the United States with Victorians adopted just one white elephant and refurbished it with donations from individuals and businesses of time, money, energy, goods, services, and Victoriana? Maybe city hall or the local hotel tax fund will help.

To help keep the house financially self-sustaining, it can be used as a museum, restaurant, town meeting hall, a place for parties, or as offices for community groups.

You will be surprised at the huge reservoir of energy, creativity, determination, and goodwill there is in your town just waiting for you to let it start flowing out into the community. The futures of Cape May, New Jersey, and Ferndale, California, were transformed just because they gussied up their Victorians.

Join or Start a Group. If you live in a town that has Victorians but no Victorian organization, start one. You will find friends and neighbors who feel as you do and have been waiting for someone like you to start the bandwagon rolling.

Put on potlucks, house tours, lectures, seminars, and demonstrations. Visit suppliers and institutions. Victorian Week, held every October in Cape May, ends with a Victorian ball. Special events are helpful both as fund-raisers and to publicize the organization.

How about doing what Chicago does: Stage an annual Painted Ladies contest to inspire homeowners to freshen up their homes? These ideas don't cost a lot of money, but they require a great deal of time, energy, and imagination. So whatever you do, encourage the Victorian spirit of play if you want your passion to be contagious. Have fun as you develop a sense of community and mission in those you enlist in the cause.

Make your group a force to be reckoned with in your town. Fight for endangered Victorians. It's been said that all that is needed for the triumph of evil is for good people to do nothing. If a Victorian worth saving is threatened, get your group to fight to save or, as a last resort, move it. Can you create a historic district or landmark the building or the block to save it?

While you may need to persist to get the attention of elected officials, they usually listen to the people who elect them. Picket, have demonstrations, have meetings, attend hearings, write letters to the editor and your elected representatives. Do whatever it takes that you won't hesitate to tell your children about.

The Alamo Square Blues

Sometimes it's not a house that's threatened, but a whole neighborhood. According to Miles's Law, where you stand depends on where you sit.

Gentrification is turning neglected downtown areas into fashionable neighborhoods. At the same time, gentrification encroaches on low-income housing. This is a problem in the Alamo Square area of San Francisco.

Crime generated by a housing project two blocks from Alamo Square became so bad that the city emptied the two buildings that were attracting miscreants. The crime rate in the area dropped 600 percent.

Now the city's Housing Authority wants to use Housing and Urban Development Funds to build more low-income housing. The Housing Authority does not have the resources to protect the present residents of the city's low-income housing or to fix more than 700 empty units.

The prospect of the city adding more low-income housing units without the ability to prevent or the means to solve the problems that afflict them, is deeply troubling to the urban pioneers in the area, who already have a crime problem caused by existing low-income housing in the neighborhood.

The homeowners are in favor of low-income housing, but they are concerned about their safety and about protecting their investments. They are also distressed at giving the false impression that they are against low-income housing, and at their inability to communicate to people in the community who need housing and who wrongly think that the homeowners are working against their interests. The irony is that the victims who suffer the most from crime in low-income housing are the tenants.

The homeowners would like the Housing Authority to use approaches that are known to minimize the problems caused by low-income housing: scatter-site housing, mixed-income housing, low-income co-ops, renter management, and market-rate housing.

To prod the city into preparing an environmental impact report, the homeowners established the Planning Association of Divisadero Street (PADS). PADS claims that if the Housing Authority were to utilize a $14-million HUD grant coupled with the city's $4-million contribution, the Housing Authority could purchase nearly as many existing units as it could provide through the process of site acquisition, demolition, and new construction.

The resolution of this dilemma may yield ideas that will help solve this problem in other cities. But whatever solution is found, let us hope that it balances the growing need for low-income housing against the incalculable value that our existing historic housing stock represents to the city as part of its architectural heritage and its tourist income.

Alamo Square is the heart of one of the most important groups of Victorian houses in the world. Recognition of the area's importance to the city and additional police protection ought to be part of any solution.

Since this is a problem that is not unique to San Francisco, wouldn't it be helpful to have a (computer?) network in which neighborhood associations could exchange ideas? An exchange of newsletters would help as would having a national forum in which to discuss questions of mutual interest.

Take care of your house. Avoid "remuddling"—that is, misguided modernization—on the exterior. When it's time to paint, make sure that the house is well prepped before it is painted. A low bid may spare your budget but not your house.

Use microanalysis to determine what colors your house was originally painted, or use Roger Moss and Gail Caskey Winkler's *Victorian Exterior Decoration* to create a historically accurate scheme, or let your own taste take over and paint your home in whatever colors you like.

Whether you use professional help or do the work yourself, your goal should be to beautify your house in a way that satisfies you and protects the house for you and for posterity.

Become the historian of your home. Of all the houses we have visited in San Francisco and around the country, only two homeowners showed us scrapbooks about the history of their homes.

When you work on your house, photograph and write about the process and the results. Put together a continuing scrapbook about the evolution of your home. A scrapbook will be helpful in carrying out future projects and it will record the history of the house, which will be of interest to your home's future owners. *The Old-House Journal* might even be interested in a story on the fruits of your labor.

Be a scout. Keep us posted. If you discover any Painted Ladies that you think we should know about for *Granddaughters of Painted Ladies* (only kidding about the title!), please send photos. We would like to have a small army of scouts around the country: Victorian buffs who know their areas well, get around a lot, and send us photos of the houses they find. If you would like to be a scout for Painted Ladies, please write to us at 1029 Jones Street, San Francisco, California, 94109. Scouts will be acknowledged in the book and will receive a free autographed copy.

Nobody will ask you to follow up on any of these suggestions. Like the homeowners who paint their houses, you will become an active member of the Victorian network as a labor of love, because you want to for your community, your family, and yourself.

One of America's amazing virtues is that if an idea has enough merit and is pursued with enough vigor, the resources needed to implement the idea will materialize. The world always steps aside for people who know where they're going. As surely as the first homeowner who created a Painted Lady led to your reading these words, you can make a bigger difference than you can imagine.

A Guide to Victorian San Francisco

The purpose of this guide is to enable San Franciscans and visitors to the city to take advantage of the city's Victorian resources. The guide is divided into two parts: suppliers and everyone else.

This selected list is part of a guidebook in progress on Victoriana in the San Francisco Bay Area to be published in 1991. Thanks in advance for dropping us a note about any group, museum, inn, artist, or supplier that you think should be included.

All telephone numbers are in the 415 area code unless otherwise noted.

I=Inexpensive, **M**=Moderate, **E**=Expensive.

The initials (AL) after a person's name indicates that he or she is a member of Artistic License, a group of top-quality artisans in period architectural and decorative art restoration.

Since craftspeople may not have showrooms and may work out of their homes, their entry may only list phone numbers. (Whether or not an address is listed, it's always best to call first.)

Bed-and-Breakfast Inns

Alamo Square Inn
719 Scott Street, 94117
922-2055. **M/E**

The Archbishop's Mansion
Alamo Square
1000 Fulton Street, 94117
563-7872. **M/E**

The Bed and Breakfast Inn
Union Street
Four Charlton Court, 94123
921-9784. **I/M**

Inn on Castro
321 Castro Street, 94114
861-0321. **M**

Chateau Tivoli
1057 Steiner, 94117
776-5462. **I/M**
Opening Summer 1990. Available now for conferences and receptions.

Inn at the Opera
Civic Center
333 Fulton, 94102
863-8400. **M/E**

The Inn San Francisco
The Mission
943 South Van Ness Avenue, 94110
641-0188. **I/M**

The Majestic
Pacific Heights
1500 Sutter at Gough, 94109
441-1100. **M/E**

The Mansion Hotel
Pacific Heights
2220 Sacramento St. 94115
929-9444. **M/E**

Nob Hill Inn
Downtown
1000 Pine Street
San Francisco, 94109
673-6080. **M**

The Red Victorian
Haight Ashbury
1665 Haight, 94117
861-7264. **M**

San Remo Hotel
North Beach
2237 Mason Street, 94133
776-8688. **I/M**

The Sherman House
Pacific Heights
2160 Green Street, 94123
563-3600. **E**

Spencer House
Buena Vista Park
1080 Haight, 94117
M

The Spreckels Mansion
Buena Vista Park
737 Buena Vista West, 94117
861-3008. **M**

Victorian Inn on the Park
Golden Gate Park
301 Lyon Street, 94117
931-1830. **M**

The Washington Square Inn
North Beach
1660 Stockton Street, 94133
981-4220. **I/M**

Dining

Big Four Restaurant
Nob Hill
Huntington Hotel
1075 California
771-1140

Cafe Majestic & Bar
Pacific Heights
1500 Sutter
441-1100

Le Castel
Presidio Heights
3235 Sacramento
921-7113

Garden Court
Downtown
Sheraton Palace Hotel, Market and New Montgomery
392-8600
Scheduled to reopen in mid-1990.

Victorian and Other Preservation Groups

Art Deco Society of California
109 Minna Street, Suite 399, 94105
552-DECO

California Historical Society
2090 Jackson, 94115
567-1848

Foundation for San Francisco's
Architectural Heritage
Haas-Lilienthal House
2007 Franklin Street, 94109
441-3000

Landmarks Preservation Advisory
Board
c/o San Francisco Planning
Department
450 McAllister, 94102
558-6345

Planning Association of
Divisadero Street
710 Broderick, 94117
565-3733

Planning Association for the
Richmond
649 14th Avenue, 94118
221-6322

Victorian Alliance
Read Gilmore
1120 South Van Ness Avenue,
94110
647-9173, or
824 Grove, 94117
824-2666

Tours

Cable Car Seminars & Tours
1111 Hamilton Avenue
Palo Alto, 94501
328-5898

City Guides' Tours
Friends of the San Francisco
Public Library, Main Library
Civic Center, 94102
558-3981

The Foundation for San Francisco's Architectural Heritage also
offers tours.

Museums

Octagon House
2645 Gough at Union, 94123
885-9797
National Society of the Colonial
Dames Headquarters.
Second and fourth Thursday and
second Sunday of each month,
12:00–3:00 P.M. Free.

Haas-Lilienthal House
2007 Franklin, 94109
441-3004
Wednesday, 12:00–4:00 P.M.; Sunday, 11:00 A.M.–4:30 P.M.; $3; $1 for
seniors and children under 12.
Weekend walks Sunday at 12:30
P.M., $3.

Whittier Mansion
2090 Jackson, 94115
567-1848
The endangered headquarters of
the California Historical Society.
Wednesday, Saturday, Sunday
1:00–4:30 P.M. House tours 1:30–
3:00 P.M., $2; $1 students and
seniors; first Saturday of the
month free.

Society of California Pioneers
Neptune Society Columbarium
#1 Loraine Court
Joseph Biernacki, Mgr.
221-1838
Tours Saturday

Civic Center
456 McAllister
861-5278
Monday through Friday,
10:00 A.M. to 4:00 P.M.

San Francisco Fire Department
Pioneer Memorial Museum
655 Presidio between Pine
and Bush
861-8000, ext. 365
Thursday through Sunday,
1:00–4:00 P.M. Free.

Classes

Tommie Veirs
Victorian decoration class
Gaslight Emporium
546-8480

UC Extension also has evening
classes on design and architecture.
Call 642-4111 for information and
a catalog.

Emporiums

Linda Blacketer, Antiques
Bayview District
1556 Revere, 94107
822-3074
Open the third Saturday of the
month, 9:00 A.M. to 1:00 P.M. and
by appointment.

Bradbury & Bradbury Art
Wallpapers
Design Service Studio and
Showroom with room sets
Pacific Heights
1925 'A' Fillmore, 94115
Bruce Bradbury (AL) founder/
owner
Paul Duchscherer (AL) Design
Service Director
922-2989
By appointment only.
Mail order address/catalogs/main
sales office and printing
facility: Bradbury & Bradbury
P.O. Box 155
Benicia, CA 94510
(707) 746-1900

Galacar & Co.
Museum Reproductions of
Wallcoverings & Fabrics
Downtown
444 Natoma, 94103
Frederick Galacar
546-3933
By appointment only.

Hoppe Imports
Statuary & Furniture
Downtown
450 Townsend, 94107
543-9795

Illustrious Lighting
Pacific Heights
1925 Fillmore, 94115
Tuesday through Saturday,
11:00 A.M. to 5:30 P.M.
John Isola (AL)
922-3133

Le Temps Perdu
Period clothing
Pacific Heights
1838 Divisadero, 94115
923-0333

San Francisco Victoriana
Architectural moldings and
plasterwork
2245 Palou Avenue, 94124
Bill Lambert, Keith Tartler (AL)
648-0313

Sunrise Specialty
The Complete Victorian Bath
2204 San Pablo Avenue
Berkeley, 94702
845-4751

The Victorian Shoppe
Needlework, ceramics, prints
Pier 39, P2, 94133
781-4770

Auction Houses

Butterfield & Butterfield
220 San Bruno Avenue, 94103
861-7500

Christie's
3516 Sacramento, 94115
346-6633

LaSalle Gallery, Inc.
1525 Union, 94123
931-9200

Harvey Clar's Gallery
5644 Telegraph
Oakland, 94609
428-0100

Artists, Craftsmen, and Consultants

Joseph Adamo
57 Bradford, 94110
821-3372

Artistic License
1925 'A' Fillmore Street, 94115
922-2854

Cynthia Baron
Interior Design and Antiques
212 Utah, 94103
282-4486

Barton Construction Co.
Iron Casting
641-0646

Bay Area Iron Works
1314 Fitzgerald Avenue, 94124
822-7844

Anne Bloomfield
Historic Research
2229 Webster, 94115
922-1063

Peter Bridgman (AL)
Wallcovering installations
653-9590

Helen Bouthell Wallcovering
Installations
254-3155

Bob Buckter
Color Consultants
3877 20th street, 94114
922-7444

J.R. Burrows
Victorian Merchant
Window, Wall, and
Floor Coverings
P.O. Box 418, Cathedral Station
Boston, MA 02118
617-455-1982

California Institute for the Restoration and Conservation Arts
3556 Sacramento, 94115
931-0444

Cirecast, Inc.
Antique hardware reproductions
380 7th Street, 94103
863-8319

Christy Cizek
Faux finishes
383-8113

Jerry Coe
Architectural and
Sculptural Metal Smith
527-2950

David Condon (AL)
Kiln Works, Architectural
Sculpture
763-5464

Allen Dragge (AL)
Reflection Studios, Leaded and
Stained Glass
652-4884

Paul Duchscherer (AL)
Architectural and Decorative Arts
Historian
Bradbury & Bradbury Design Service Director
922-2989

Robert Dufort (AL)
Magic Brush, Inc.
Painting and refinishing
1500 'B' Davidson Avenue, 94122
641-8622

Franklin Design
2026 California, 94109
922-3400

Anton Fuetsch (AL)
Wood Carver
526-6344

Haas Wood & Ivory Works
Ornamentation
44 Clementina, 94105
421-8273

John Isola (AL)
Illustrious Lighting
1925 Fillmore, 94115
922-3133

Erik Kramvik (AL)
Design & Fine Woodworking
Architectural Restoration
333-4932

Lorna Kollmeyer
Ornamental Plaster
661-8211

Little/Raidl Design Studios
Custom Art Glass in the
Tiffany manner
49 Hartford, 94114
552-3557

Jim Mannix
San Francisco Renovation
921-6170

The Miniature Mart
Ellen and John Blauer
1870 Octavia Street, 94109
563-8745

David John Modell (AL)
Architectural Restoration Design
239-0585

Joni Monnich (AL)
Lilyguild—Decorative Painted
Finishes
724-4405

Bruce Nelson (AL)
Local Color, Painting Restoration
398-8018

Ocean Sash & Door
3154 17th Street, 94110
863-1256/0792

Jill Pilaroscia (AL)
Architectural Colour
Interor and exterior paint schemes
861-8086

Gail Redman (AL)
Fine Wood Turning
431-1595

Mark Egeland
Return to Splendor
Wallpaper installation, graining,
marbleizing
530-1051

Stephen Rynerson (AL)
Period Design—
Architectural Design
525-9135

Rick Schaefer
Wood ornament, moldings
863-0248

John Seecamp
Stainer, woodwork, and graining
824-3493

Steven F. Stevens
Stained Glass Studio
1380 Bush, 94109
885-5236
By appointment only.

Tree Lovers' Floors, Inc.
230 Ritch
Oakland, 94609
777-1673

Thomas Tisch-Andreas Lehmann
(AL)
Cut Glass
465-7158

Phil Waen (AL)
Classic Illumination—Lighting
849-1842

Paul Winans (AL)
Winans Construction, General
Contractor
653-7288

Bob Winebarger (AL)
Furniture maker
527-8397

Winfield Design Associates
Wallcoverings
2690 Harrison, 94110
647-6787

George Zaffle (AL)
Zaffle Painting Studio
621-7653

Painters

Cal Crew
Gustavo Caldavelli
731-9292

Clark Chelsey
Chelsey Painters
644-3031

Classic Strokes
187 Coleridge, 94110
647-6224

Color Quest
Paul Kensinger
1793 McAllister, 94115
921-1121

Concepts in Color
Aryae Levy
647-7070

Esther Canaletich
San Francisco Renaissance
Painting
2000 Bridgeway
Sausalito, 94965
331-8252

Russell Epstein Painting &
Decorating Co.
3420 Market Street, #11, 94114
826-0493

Butch Kardum Painting &
Color Design
210 San Jose Avenue
824-1623

Local Color Painting &
Restoration
Bruce Nelson (AL)
990 Greenhill Road
Mill Valley 94941
389-8018

Mirage
Bill Weber & Tony Klaas
828-9284

Pago Painting
Brian Moloney
753-6064

Ron McCambridge
Peacock Painting Company
506 Chenery, 94131
584-1816

Precision Painters
690 Arkansas, 94107
626-3131

San Francisco Renaissance Color
Design
Tony Canaletich
921-5197

Strokes Design
282-2141

The Painted Ladies Revisited
Honorable Mentions

Our approach to finding houses was to ride around town, talk to the Victorian network, and trust our instincts about what we found. Different eyes would have made different choices.

We found houses that we couldn't shoot because of trees, wires, or weathering. Some of the houses we shot looked fine when we saw them, but, despite Doug Keister's skill, they didn't look as good in a four-by-five-inch transparency.

Sometimes the colors were a factor, sometimes it was the way light hit the building. Sometimes we disagreed with each other and our editor about what to include. Sometimes we photographed a house and then found a better example of the color scheme or the architecture.

We photographed the following houses, and while they didn't make the final cut, they deserve Honorable Mention. We would also like to thank those owners who helped us in photographing them and provided information on them. We apologize for the letdown that occurred when the hopes we engendered about being in the book were dashed. Maybe next time.

Downtown: 2502 Leavenworth.

Pacific Heights: 2447 Washington, 2527 Washington, 2608 Sacramento, 2187 California, 2815 Pine, 1909 Baker, 1803 Laguna, 1809 Gough, 1831 Steiner, 1406 Post.

Western Addition: 1801 Ellis, 1421 Golden Gate, 709 Scott, 722 Steiner, 503 Divisadero, 706 Broderick, 623 Baker, 627 Baker, 236 Ashbury, 82 Webster, 170 Page.

Haight Ashbury: 1056 Page, 118 Broderick, 508 Cole, 510 Cole, 722 Cole, 733 Cole, 755 Cole, 752 Clayton, 1215 Waller.

Noe Valley: 167 Noe, 1065 Noe, 1190 Noe, 3753 17th, 725 Castro, 563 and 567 Liberty, 576 Liberty, 3881 21st, 3845 24th, 1374 Sanchez.

The Mission: 49 Hill, 53 and 59 Hill, 15 Liberty, 1211 Guerrero, 1253 Guerrero, 1327 Guerrero, 701 Shotwell, 754 and 760 Shotwell, 1059 Florida, 1328 York.

Glossary of Wall Ornamentation

by Bruce Bradbury

Border: a decorative band of ornament in the domestic interior, usually nine inches or less in height.

Corner fans: designs that radiate inward from the corner of the ceiling decoration.

Cornice: molding at the top of the walls of a room, usually of plaster or wood, between walls and ceilings.

Cove or coving: concave molding or curved surface forming the junction between walls and ceiling.

Crown decoration: an encircling band of ornament that unites wall and ceiling as a decorative whole. It usually includes a picture rail, frieze, cornice, and enrichment area.

Dado: lower portion of the wall of a room, decorated differently from the upper section. When made of wood, it is usually called a wainscot. The dado can be up to three feet from the floor and is usually topped by a wooden molding or paper border. "Fill" paper fills in the main upper wall. Then there is a frieze on top. Between the filler and frieze is a picture rail or plate rail. Indian matting is sometimes used for the dado; so is Japanese imitation leather and Lincrusta.

Dado rail: a railing of wood, wallpaper border, or stenciled band that separates the dado from the upper wall. Wooden rails were intended to protect the wall surface from damage when chairs were placed around the walls, hence it's often called a chair-rail.

Decoupage: a technique of decorating a surface with paper cutouts.

Enrichment: a pattern, often small and geometric, richer in coloring than would normally be used on a full wall. It may be used as a dado in wall panels, to ornament coving, or as a ceiling filling.

Filling: (1) the main portion of wall between the dado and frieze; (2) any wall or ceiling portion between two borders.

Frieze: a decorative horizontal band along the upper part of a wall or the design intended for such a space.

Hue: the dimension of color as it moves through the spectrum—red, orange, yellow, green, etc.

Picture rail: molding often eighteen inches below the cornice from which framed pictures can be suspended without damaging the wall surface.

Plate rail: a broad shelflike molding sometimes located below the picture rail but often used in place of it. The top of the shelf is grooved to hold decorative plates.

Polychrome: to decorate in many or various colors, from the Greek: *poly*—many, *chrome*—color.

Shade: a quality of color as it moves from light to dark; for example, pink to red burgundy (*see also* hue).

Wainscot: *see* dado.

A dazzling display of Bradbury & Bradbury Wallpapers may be seen by appointment only in their San Francisco showroom (1925'A' Fillmore, 922-2989), which, with the help of John Isola of Illustrious Lighting downstairs, has been furnished like a Victorian home.

Bibliography

Books

Bruce, Curt, and Aidala, Thomas. *Great Houses of San Francisco*. New York: Alfred A. Knopf, 1974.

A Decorator. *Victorian Interior Decoration: The Paper Hanger, Painter, Grainer, and Decorator's Assistant*. 1879. Watkins Glen, N.Y.: American Life Books, 1977.

Dresser, Christopher. *The Art of Decorative Design*. 1862. Watkins Glen, N.Y.: American Life Foundation, 1977.

Gebhard, David. *The Guide to Architecture in San Francisco and Northern California*. Layton, Utah: Gibbs M. Smith/Perigrine Smith Books, 1985.

Grow, Lawrence, and von Zwek, Dina. *American Victorian: A Style and Source Book*. New York: The Main Street Press/Harper & Row, 1984.

Hansen, Gladys. *San Francisco Almanac*. San Francisco: Chronicle Books, 1975.

Howard, Hugh, for Home Renovation Associates. *How Old Is This House? A Skeleton Key to Dating and Identifying Three Centuries of American Houses*. New York: The Noonday Press, 1989.

Kemp, Jim. *Victorian Revival in Interior Design*. New York: Quarto Marketing Ltd./Simon & Schuster, 1985.

Leopold, Allison Kyle, and Heyert, Elizabeth. *Victorian Splendor: Re-Creating America's 19th-Century Interiors*. New York: Stewart, Tabori & Chang, 1985.

Moss, Roger W. *Lighting for Historic Buildings*: A *Guide to Selecting Reproductions*. Washington, D.C.: The Preservation Press, 1988.

Moss, Roger W., and Winkler, Gail Caskey. *Victorian Exterior Decoration: How to Paint Your Nineteenth-Century American House Historically*. New York: Henry Holt, 1987.

Muthesius, Stephen. *The High Victorian Movement in Architecture 1850–1870*. London: Routledge, Kegan Paul, 1972.

Omsted, Roger, and Watkins, T. H. *Here Today: San Francisco's Architectural Heritage*. Photographs by Morley Baer and others. San Francisco: The Junior League of San Francisco/Chronicle Books, 1986.

Rosensteil, Helen von, and Winkler, Gail Caskey. *Floor Coverings for Historic Buildings*. Washington, D.C.: Preservation Press, 1988.

Waldhorn, Judith Lynch, and Woodbridge, Sally B. *Victoria's Legacy: Tours of San Francisco Bay Area Architecture*. San Francisco: 101 Productions, 1978.

Wellikoff, Alan. *The American Historical Supply Catalogue*. New York: Schocken Books, 1984.

Winkler, Gail Caskey, and Moss, Roger W. *Victorian Interior Decoration: American Interiors 1830–1900*. New York: LCA Associates/Henry Holt, 1986.

Woodbridge, Sally B. *California Architecture*. San Francisco: Chronicle Books, 1988.

Periodicals

Architectural Digest, P.O. Box 10040, Des Moines, Iowa 50340; 5900 Wilshire Blvd., Los Angeles, California 90036; (800) 421-4448.

The Old-House Journal, Old-House Journal Corp; 435 Ninth Street, Brooklyn, New York 11215; (718) 636-4514.

Victoria Magazine, The Hearst Corporation, 1700 Broadway, New York, New York 10019.

Victorian Homes, Renovator's Supply, Inc., Miller Falls, Massachusetts 01349.

Victorian Sampler, P.O. Box 546, 707 Kantz Rd., St. Charles, Illinois 61744.

Notes on the Photographs

After traveling to forty-four states in 1986 to photograph *Daughters of Painted Ladies* for Elizabeth and Michael, I became a San Francisco commuter for *The Painted Ladies Revisited*. Photographing locally for a span of a year enabled me to pick the best type of light and weather to photograph the houses. The main problem of photographing Victorians in San Francisco is the multitude of wires that enter the picture when the camera is backed up far enough to include the whole house. Wires interfering with the planes of the image have always been a pet peeve with me, and I will go to almost any length to rid the photograph of them. Moving closer to the houses, tilting the camera up, and using a wide-angle lens produces too much distortion; thus, the only solution is to get very high in the air and shoot the houses straight on with medium-wide lenses. Norm Fisher of California Photo Service gave me the solution by providing me with a ten-foot ladder tripod. Getting high off the ground enabled me to eliminate most of the wire problems plus get some interesting perspectives of the houses. This, combined with using different lenses and photographing in a variety of lighting and weather conditions, makes for what I hope are visually exciting photographs.

A Sinar F 4x5 view camera was used for all of the photos. Lenses used were a 65mm Nikkor, 90mm Schneider Super Angulon, 120mm Nikkor, 135mm Schneider Planar, and a 180mm Schneider Symmar. A 1A or 1B filter was used for houses photographed in full or slanting sunlight. A Tiffen 812 filter was used for backlit houses or overcast days. Ektachrome 6122 daylight film was used for most of the photographs although Ektachrome Plus 6105 was used when I determined that a red boost was needed. Composition was checked using Polaroid Type 59 color film.

With Michael acting as stylist and art director, we embarked on documenting some of the fabulous interiors of San Francisco's Victorians. Except for some detail shots, the 65mm and 90mm wide-angle lenses were used throughout. Lighting was provided by Novatron flash units equipped with lite dome and white dome reflectors. Varying degrees of ambient light were added to provide the necessary warmth for a Victorian room. Once again, Polaroid Type 59 was used to check image composition and lighting.

I should like to thank Michael and Elizabeth for giving me an opportunity to participate in the making of a beautiful book. Many thanks go to Norm Fisher, LaVerne Fisher, and Steve (Mr. E-6) Grodin of California Photo Service for their encouragement and support of the project. Additional thanks go to Bill and Dr. Bob for putting me back together and to HP for keeping me there.

Clockwise from top: Doug Keister, Steve Grodin, Laverne Fisher, and Norm Fisher.

Authors' Biographies

Elizabeth Pomada and Michael Larsen worked in publishing in New York before moving to San Francisco, where they started the Bay Area's oldest literary agency in 1972. They created *California Publicity Outlets* (1972), now called *Metro California Media*.

Their first book on Victorians, *Painted Ladies: San Francisco's Resplendent Victorians*, was published in 1978, and is now in its fifteenth printing. The American Institute of Graphic Arts chose it as one of the best design books of the year.

Painted Ladies started a national trend toward beautifying Victorians. This led to the publication of *Daughters of Painted Ladies: America's Resplendent Victorians* (1987), now in its third printing, which *Publishers Weekly* selected as one of the best books of the year.

Elizabeth Pomada wrote *Places to Go with Children in Northern California* (1973), now in its seventh revised edition, and also writes about food, culture, and travel.

Writer's Digest Books published Michael Larsen's books: *How to Write a Book Proposal* (1985), now in its fourth printing; *Literary Agents: How to Get and Work with the Right One for You* (1986), now in its second printing; and his collaboration with Hal Bennett, *How to Write with a Collaborator* (1988). Michael's next opus, *The Worry Bead Book: The World's Oldest & Simplest Way to Beat Stress*, is being published in fall 1989 by St. Martin's Press. Since travel is a passion, the two have hopes for a *Distant Cousins of Painted Ladies* in the future.

Douglas Keister got his start in photography in 1964 after finding some discarded but usable Kodak chemicals in a neighbor's garbage can. He took his first photographs with his parents' Brownie Hawkeye camera and made contact prints using two pieces of glass and a lamp. After his early training in Nebraska, he moved to California in 1969. His photographs, taken primarily with a view camera, have appeared in numerous publications and are also owned by collectors.

California Photo Service published his book *Driftwood Whimsy: The Sculptures of the Emeryville Mudflats* in 1985. He took the photographs for Elizabeth and Michael's book *Daughters of Painted Ladies*, published by E. P. Dutton in 1987, and is working as a commercial, advertising, and architectural photographer in Oakland, California. During Keister's spare time he tends to his Uncle Milton's Giant Ant Farm.